D1736840

PHOENIX

In loving memory of our brother
Philippe Zdar

LIBERTÉ, ÉGALITÉ, PHOENIX!

Deck d'Arcy, Laurent Brancowitz, Thomas Mars, Christian Mazzalai
An Oral History by Laura Snapes

RIZZOLI
NEW YORK

New York · Paris · London · Milan

LIBERTÉ, ÉGALITÉ, PHOENIX!

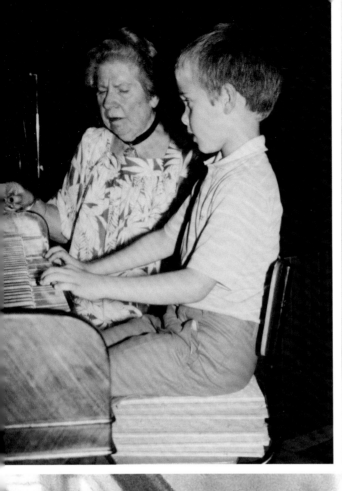

EARLY DAYS

Phoenix: DECK D'ARCY. LAURENT BRANCOWITZ. THOMAS MARS. CHRISTIAN MAZZALAI.
Other voices: PHILIPPE ASCOLI, Source Records. CHAG BARATIN, friend. ROB COUDERT, friend. JEAN-LOUIS CROQUET, Thomas's father. NICOLAS GODIN, Air. URSEL MAZZALAI, Christian and Branco's mother. LAURENCE MULLER, Virgin France legal and business affairs/Phoenix's future manager. CÉDRIC PLANCY, friend/Boxon. JASON SCHWARTZMAN, actor/musician. MARC TEISSIER DU CROS, Source Records. SÉBASTIEN TELLIER, musician. MARIE-CHRISTINE VIDAL, Deck's mother. PEDRO WINTER, Daft Punk's manager.

LAURENT BRANCOWITZ: When Chris and I were very young, in Italy, our father's cousin played guitar. I remember suddenly understanding that you could play a song that you heard on the radio. I could see the effect it had on my father. He could cry sometimes, and my father would never cry, except listening to music. So, very young, I knew there was a special power to this thing.

CHRISTIAN MAZZALAI: I only played music because Branco took guitar lessons for two months, then quit and bought an "Easy Beatles" book. He taught me one chord every month, so I learned very slowly.

DECK D'ARCY: I started piano with my great-grandma, who was a piano teacher. Her husband was an opera singer. My grandma on the other side played violin with her—that's how my parents met. But I didn't discover music through my family.

THOMAS MARS: My older brother David played me a lot of music. He's nine years older. He'd take me to shows: I went to see the Cure when I was eleven, and then a weird mix between arena events and small, unappealing punk gigs.

LAURENT BRANCOWITZ: Chris and I have the same name, Mazzalai. Brancowitz is on my grandmother's side. It's the name I used when I was looking for an artist's name. Everyone called me Branco. Our parents had a very small but very good record collection.

CHRISTIAN MAZZALAI: Simon and Garfunkel, Brazilian music, João Gilberto.

Italian music, of course. And the Beatles. *A Hard Day's Night* was translated in Italian: All for One, *Tutti per Uno*.

LAURENT BRANCOWITZ: When I was ten, I got the cassette of *Thriller* for Christmas. This was our first record from our generation. Chris and I would listen to it every day. The first thing I was a real fan of was the B-52s. I never read an interview with them. Anything I knew about them was just from the liner notes, which was very important for protecting your own reality. At fourteen, I was really into *Sign o' the Times*. One summer night, I heard a bunch of older kids outside my window. They were playing "The Cross" on guitar. A few years later, I realized it was Nicolas from Air. We were living in the same neighborhood but we never crossed paths.

CHRISTIAN MAZZALAI: The first counterculture I discovered was Pixies. It was '88, so I was twelve. I hated it. Branco said, "It's normal, first you will hate it, but then you will love it." The biggest shock was My Bloody Valentine, *Isn't Anything*. It was fantastic, but I couldn't believe it was made on purpose. It felt like there was a problem with the stereo. It's so mysterious!

LAURENT BRANCOWITZ: I started playing guitar late, at fifteen, sixteen. I didn't want to be a musician, I just thought it would be so cool to know how to play a song, just like a magic trick. We were very self-taught. Once in a while there was something good on T.V., so if we were lucky we would see the position of the fingers on the fretboard. Even though we were twenty minutes from Paris, that world was so remote. Me and Chris were very bad skateboarders—we knew that tricks existed, but we never saw anyone do any. Having someone teach us was not even possible. Their existence was like a rumor.

URSEL MAZZALAI: From a very young age, Laurent would say, "I don't want to work with colleagues in an office in the future." He wanted to be a rock star or a comic performer. Christian wanted to have a stationery shop with colored pencils and books.

CHRISTIAN MAZZALAI: We were very close but we had crazy, physical fights. Branco won almost every time. I only won once. He fell from the window. I pushed him from the bed. It was very violent. But we were close. Just extreme.

LAURENT BRANCOWITZ: My parents were very concerned about our future. But we weren't into drugs. I realized that the codes of rebellion were very conformist. I felt very angry about it. All the first records I listened to were filled with this intention of trying to destroy the rules.

URSEL MAZZALAI: Contrary to their father, I was really worried. I didn't sleep for months. I was picturing them playing music and sleeping on the streets.

DECK D'ARCY: I went to school with Chris from six to ten. I was living in Bois d'Arcy. It was a bit dodgy, so my parents put me in a different school in le Chesnay. The first time Chris and I met is a bit blurry. We played soccer in my garden.

CHRISTIAN MAZZALAI: Deck was always in the top three at school. Once, I was better than him. His parents were teachers. They wanted him to go to a very good school, Lycée Hoche. So from ten to fourteen, we didn't see each other. That's when he met Thomas in Versailles.

THOMAS MARS: Versailles is fake money, it's cheap, it's bourgeois, pretty right-wing, Catholic. There were royalists. There was this kid whose surname was le Roi—the King. He was born to be a royalist. I couldn't stand him. I never went to his place but the rumor was that he had posters of himself in his bedroom. He always wore white denim. The lame revenge was to put Nutella on the seat of his Vespa. I don't know if he ever sat in it. I think Cédric and I were probably the only two atheists in our Catholic school. My mom was very protective of Cédric because he was the only kid who wasn't white.

LAURENT BRANCOWITZ: Versailles and le Chesnay, where Chris and I lived, are totally different. Le Chesnay was a new city very influenced by American urbanism, built around one of Europe's first malls. It's a very rare place in France. A new city, kind of rootless. And our parents are foreigners. Next to Versailles, where people live among heritage, we are the Galapagos Islands.

DECK D'ARCY: In '87, Thomas and I became friends halfway through the year. We started talking about tennis. He was great at tennis. I was really bad.

JEAN-LOUIS CROQUET: I have pictures of Thomas breaking his racket because he was losing. He doesn't like to lose.

DECK D'ARCY: We talked a lot about music because Thomas's brother David knew all the cool bands.

THOMAS MARS: I had a Prince show on V.H.S. I would pray in front of it. I never believed in God, but I was just so into it.

DECK D'ARCY: Thomas was making a lot of tapes with customized sleeves. He made me a great compilation of *Sign o' the Times*–era Prince. We got more into Joy Division when we were twelve, thirteen.

CÉDRIC PLANCY: We were listening to French punk bands, the Sex Pistols.

THOMAS MARS: Every guy in our school was a square. The only guy you could talk to about music was obsessed with Bach. No one was listening to music. That was scary.

CHRISTIAN MAZZALAI: I didn't know Versailles until I was fifteen. I'm still shocked by how different the people in my class were.

JEAN-LOUIS CROQUET: Thomas was only interested by music. He told me he would rather spend his life in a very uninteresting job in music than be an architect or a doctor.

THOMAS MARS: The first time Deck came over, he played music with me and Cédric. I had a drum kit that I couldn't play. Deck had a tiny keyboard. Cédric would sing and play my brother's bass.

DECK D'ARCY: We plugged the keyboard into the stereo at maximum volume and it instantly blew up. We had one song, a one-note song. Just the physical experience of loudness was enough.

THOMAS MARS: We had to wait a month for it to be fixed. It was a good frustrating experience. We practiced in my parents' basement whenever we could after school. Cédric was around but Deck wasn't always allowed to come. By then it was Deck, myself, a French kid called Xavier, and Viktor Stoïchita, a Romanian kid who had left the Ceaușescu regime. He was super nice and perfectly weird. He told us all the time that he would watch erotic movies on TV with his dad on Sunday nights. We were like, "We are *not* going to his place..."

DECK D'ARCY: Viktor could play better than me. He was listening to commercial music when we met him. With us he discovered post-punk. He became a communist and got really politically engaged.

THOMAS MARS: We had our own language. I'm sure our parents must have been concerned, because we'd use twelve words over and over.

MARIE-CHRISTINE VIDAL: They were not very talkative at all, actually. Deck spent hours at his desk playing air drums, his head in the clouds.

DECK D'ARCY: The first name we got ourselves was Boxon, which means mess.

CÉDRIC PLANCY: Thomas's father was saying we sounded like a big mess. He always had funny expressions like this.

CHRISTIAN MAZZALAI: I saw a video of their first concert; they were twelve. Thomas had a full drum kit but he didn't know how to play, so he only played the snare. Very minimal. And two keyboards. They were into Bauhaus. This band was fantastic, but with a catastrophic singer.

CHAG BARATIN: In France, *collège* is age ten to fourteen, and then if your *collège* doesn't have the higher class, from fourteen to eighteen, you go to a different school for the last three years.

CHRISTIAN MAZZALAI: When I was fourteen, I take the bus on the first day of school and who do I see? Deck. "Hey!" I could see he didn't want to talk to me. He was thinking I was not cool any more.

DECK D'ARCY: I hadn't really seen him for a long time. Puberty, everything's changing. I had it quite early, but he was still looking like a kid. He jumps in and I was like, "Oh shit." I was listening to music and we couldn't avoid each other.

CHRISTIAN MAZZALAI: "What are you listening to?"

DECK D'ARCY: "The Pixies."

CHRISTIAN MAZZALAI: "Ah, you know the Pixies?" After one minute, we were talking. At that time, no one knew the Pixies.

DECK D'ARCY: It totally changed my view of him. He had changed a lot in four years. He had a strong personality, strong sense of humor, very positive. We became friends again. He already knew the Stone Roses and all the bands we were about to discover through Branco.

CHRISTIAN MAZZALAI: We went into school. There was one black sheep: Thomas. Long hair. He was so shy, he couldn't even walk in the streets, he had to run. After one minute, we were best friends.

THOMAS MARS: We would talk about our brothers' music taste. Branco would ask Chris, "There's no way he knows Moose!" Chris was going back and saying, "He does!" And Branco said, "He's okay." It was really my brother talking to his brother.

LAURENT BRANCOWITZ: I could see they weren't the usual dorks. They stood out very vividly.

DECK D'ARCY: Cédric came in as a guitarist—the lineup was Thomas, Cédric, and me. We had gone more American—we started doing Pixies covers. We were looking for a singer so we found a guy at school, Jean. He wasn't a singer at all, and he was really into the Doors and liked to rehearse barefoot. But in Versailles, you had no choice.

CHRISTIAN MAZZALAI: They told me, "If you want to come see us, we are playing on Saturday." I could play "Where Is My Mind?" with a capo. They did a cover of it already. It was a little... rearranged.

DECK D'ARCY: He barely knew how to play. He knew two chords. He couldn't do it standing. But we didn't care. He was cool and he had a cool sound.

CHRISTIAN MAZZALAI: It was the first time I had played in a band. Super loud.

DECK D'ARCY: At fifteen, you put everything maximum. We were not into subtlety.

CHRISTIAN MAZZALAI: Everything was stupidly muffled. They had lagged the room in foam so it was super dead. That's why our sound is very dry.

DECK D'ARCY: Thomas, Cédric, and me talked for two seconds. "What do we do?" "Okay, we take him."

CHRISTIAN MAZZALAI: I came back home and told my parents and Branco: "I'm in a band!" I was so happy. The timing was perfect. I never knew what to do at the weekends, I always felt like a loser. But then I was born. So every week we were dreaming of this moment, these five hours a week: *What are we gonna do?*

DECK D'ARCY: Without Thomas's parents we probably wouldn't have the band. They let us rehearse at their place with very loud music. They're pretty open-minded.

MARIE-CHRISTINE VIDAL: It was so loud you could hear them from the street! All my respect to Thomas's parents for bearing this volume for so long.

THOMAS MARS: The pipes go right into every bedroom and somehow amplify the sound. I think the only place where you're safe is my parents' bathroom.

JEAN-LOUIS CROQUET: I suppose we were very cool parents with our children. I think my duty was to help them be happy.

THOMAS MARS: My mom is German and she comes from World War II trauma.

The German philosophy after the war was, "It's forbidden to forbid." So everything was allowed at my place.

CHAG BARATIN: Thomas lived in his own kind of flat in the house; his friends could come. His parents gave him a lot of freedom.

CHRISTIAN MAZZALAI: His walls were covered in mirrored paper, like in Warhol's Factory. We were writing lyrics on the mirror of the bathroom with lipstick.

LAURENT BRANCOWITZ: Thomas was a bit raised by wolves. He had a period of having bratty tendencies. He was the kind of kid who had a small motorcycle when he was twelve. State-of-the-art video games. A very bad loser. I think he had some kind of personality epiphany. Maybe Deck and Chris were an influence.

CÉDRIC PLANCY: Chris was always making a joke, but with a bit of seriousness, "Oh, you with your money."

THOMAS MARS: Before I met Chris, I was kind of braggy. And he put me back in my place. There's something very judgemental about him, but in a way that helped you define who you can be as a teenager.

CHRISTIAN MAZZALAI: Thomas wasn't from a posh family. His father was a son of a hairdresser. But he was a self-made man, so he bought a crazy house. It's like a mini Château de Versailles.

THOMAS MARS: The hotel of the actual palace was at the end of the street, and every day someone would come into our house with their luggage thinking this was the hotel.

CHRISTIAN MAZZALAI: In the summer, the palace had a fireworks display every weekend. On Sunday morning, they would soundcheck in the palace

gardens, testing Lully and Rameau ultra-loud on the P.A. while we were playing soccer in the garden. It's very Versailles. We loved it. We used to climb inside at night.

DECK D'ARCY: Our parents made friends. They're still close. Back then they were totally sure we were drug addicts. It was so annoying: they would pump each other for information, then my mom would come back and check my pockets. We were never into drugs—we hated how the kids at our school felt they were so cool for doing them. We were just into smoking. Also our parents were sure Thomas and I were lovers. We were sleeping in the same bed sometimes. But it was this or the floor.

MARIE-CHRISTINE VIDAL: I was secretly and thoroughly checking Deck's pockets and his arms, but I was not very subtle. He noticed and teased me.

URSEL MAZZALAI: I never thought they were drug addicts, but I thought they were lovers because they were always together, day and night, in Thomas's basement. They were dirty boys! Especially Christian. He didn't like water. But the four of them were very sweet, very respectable.

MARIE-CHRISTINE VIDAL: After school, they would literally run to their rehearsal space to save minutes of practice.

THOMAS MARS: Friday nights were important because you knew we had like two, three hours before Deck's parents would pick him up.

DECK D'ARCY: We took it seriously but with a fifteen-year-old's mindset: that your life is dedicated to music, but you don't know exactly what that means.

CHRISTIAN MAZZALAI: We have recordings of our rehearsals. It's either a big noise or screaming. Always me and Thomas fighting about details. I remember jumping his drums, a physical fight.

DECK D'ARCY: There were lots of physical fights between Thomas and Chris because they were both shrimps: very skinny, small, like children's bodies. Cédric and me were bigger and stronger, so we didn't physically fight them because it wouldn't be fair.

THOMAS MARS: We didn't even dare to be physical, we just threw things. I threw a tennis ball at his guitar.

CHRISTIAN MAZZALAI: After two years there was no more fights.

DECK D'ARCY: The band became much more guitar-based. I started playing bass. We fired Jean in a very cheap way, pretending we couldn't make practice.

CHRISTIAN MAZZALAI: When we were fifteen, we were in Thomas's country house in Burgundy for the weekend and saw a documentary about the making of *Sgt. Pepper*. We were traumatized.

DECK D'ARCY: George Martin was using a four-track recorder. It was a big shock: *That's how you layer stuff.* The week after, we bought the cheapest four-track.

THOMAS MARS: We were so judgemental about everything. If a band had not even the wrong guitar, but held it at the wrong angle, we were like, *nope*.

CHRISTIAN MAZZALAI: Every month we discovered something new. Dionne Warwick, Burt Bacharach, Bob Dylan. So many revelations.

LAURENT BRANCOWITZ: I wouldn't say they were really good. But there was already a kind of vision compared to the other local bands, who were playing U2 and Red Hot Chili Pepper covers.

MARIE-CHRISTINE VIDAL: I was not very convinced by their first recordings.

THOMAS MARS: There was a *les Inrocks* festival. One night was Lush, Blur, and Pulp, which Chris went to. I went to the other one: Ocean Colour Scene, Ride. Branco went to both.

LAURENT BRANCOWITZ: I met my wife on the first night. We've been together ever since.

ROB COUDERT: I was playing in a P-funk band that often performed in the Versailles area—I lived in Marly le Roi, where Louis XIV had his countryside house. They came to a show and I think they were impressed by our quite ambitious playing and performance. We had a full horn section, who ended up playing on *United*.

THOMAS MARS: We all loved hanging out with Rob. He always got it.

CHRISTIAN MAZZALAI: We played very few shows.

THOMAS MARS: We never wanted to be a live band.

ROB COUDERT: I saw them performing one of their first shows as Phoenix, in Versailles. For some reason, I have no memory at all of the music itself, but I remember they were a balance of extreme amateurism and this real strong power, something like an aura, like they were born to be rock stars.

CHRISTIAN MAZZALAI: I saw footage from '92 that my father filmed at Fête de la Musique. It was us, another band, and Darlin'. It's fun because it's very

no-compromises, but otherwise I'm not sure it's very good. We were trying to not look at the crowd. French shoegazing.

LAURENT BRANCOWITZ: When I was seventeen, I was looking for a band. I looked at the ads in Danceteria, one of the few good record stores in Paris. The music these ads mentioned was always really depressing. But there was one that was hand-written and very well designed. It listed the Velvet Underground, Spacemen 3, the Beach Boys, 13th Floor Elevators. The Beach Boys didn't have this status they have now. This combination stood out immediately. I'd never answered an ad. I called Guy-Man, and we met in a McDonald's in front of the Luxembourg gardens. It was 1 January, 1992. We were still at school. We were very bad musicians, but it was more about the friendship. I discovered a lot of music from him. He had a very strong sense of aesthetics very young, which was pretty rare.

CHRISTIAN MAZZALAI: Guy-Man told me and Branco that the best album by Iggy Pop was *Kill City*.

LAURENT BRANCOWITZ: Then I met his friend, Thomas Bangalter. Guy-Man was very suffering and full of teenage angst. True, metaphysical suffering! And Thomas was more joyful, more rational. His father was a musician. So he knew how you make records. We did a little cassette demo, an original and a cover of the Beach Boys' "Darlin,'" so we called the band Darlin'. There was a Stereolab concert. My mission was to hand this tape to Tim Gane. He contacted us and released those tracks on a split, double seven-inch with one band per side. It felt like having a platinum record, even if it was a pressing of maybe five hundred copies.

CHRISTIAN MAZZALAI: They only had one review, which was very bad. But in a way, it's a success.

LAURENT BRANCOWITZ: *Melody Maker* called us "a daft, punky mess." It wasn't true, but the name stuck. Just having a review was cool. We only played two or three shows. Darlin' never officially broke up because it was never officially created. It was just very natural. They were into the beginnings of rave culture in Paris, and I really wasn't. Their first album was instantly successful. I was really happy to see close friends living a cool adventure. Then I became more involved with Phoenix.

DECK D'ARCY: Cédric left. We never really understood why. It was sad because he was our best friend.

THOMAS MARS: His father went back to Martinique. That was a very troubled moment for him.

CÉDRIC PLANCY: There was a lot of pressure on me. It's difficult to say, "Guys, I'm leaving." It's more like you create a distance. I really wanted to learn English better, so I went to London, worked in restaurants, D.J.'ed at parties.

LAURENT BRANCOWITZ: An aspiring filmmaker friend found a stock of film to make a small movie. I said I wanted to do the music. I knew my brother's band was available, so I asked if we could do it together. Maybe before that I was producing one of their tracks, imagining I was Phil Spector, even though I had zero technical knowledge. That's how we first played music together, doing music for this movie that we never saw.

DECK D'ARCY: The music was influenced by *Pat Garrett and Billy the Kid* by Bob Dylan.

CHRISTIAN MAZZALAI: It was just the four of us from then on.

THOMAS MARS: The only thing we were into was music and being together. We wanted to do everything ourselves, like the Beastie Boys and Grand Royal. We would dress up to go to the studio. We took this photo of us in suits, dressing up like executives going to work. We wanted this to be our job so much.

CHRISTIAN MAZZALAI: We had a name every two weeks. Señoritas. Love Boat.

CHAG BARATIN: They played at Thomas's parents' wedding as the Mariachis. I was doing the sound.

LAURENT BRANCOWITZ: We all had a lot of nicknames. Deck's real name is Frédéric Moulin. Thomas's last name is Croquet. At some point he had the nickname Blanche.

THOMAS MARS: There was no reason for picking Mars other than that it sounded good. We named the studio Royal Riot on some tapes, the Sun King studio on others.

CHRISTIAN MAZZALAI: Maybe '95 was when we picked a name. Thomas and I were in the same bed. He went, "Phoenix?" I said, "Ah, oui." He doesn't remember.

LAURENT BRANCOWITZ: We had a heroic vision of what our career should be, and it had a lot to do with the fact that we were really isolated. The Beatles had twelve records in ten years and they were all perfect. It was very clear and pure because we didn't see all the compromises they had to make. And so our vision of an artist's life was really a vision of legend.

THOMAS MARS: We thought we were the next Beatles. My dad said we were more snobbish than the snobs. Except we were even more distant than the snobs: We wouldn't say, "We're the next biggest band in the world," like a British band would. We just wouldn't even vaguely interact with people.

CHAG BARATIN: I never had any doubts that they couldn't do it.

THOMAS MARS: Writing in English was being snobbier than the snobs, but also French was too revealing. English was the perfect way to hide. Also in French, it was hard to reinvent the language. Dylan, Hank Williams—we loved that kind of songwriting.

LAURENT BRANCOWITZ: We had this dream of writing for Johnny Cash. We asked him to remix us. We copied a letter that Truffaut wrote to Kubrick to maximize our chances. Obviously, he didn't reply.

DECK D'ARCY: We had no idea how to make the band work. We were just sure it would happen. We didn't even have songs. After Branco joined, the four of us went on vacation to Thomas's country house. We stayed in the barn and wrote songs. One is on *United*, "Party Time."

THOMAS MARS: Deck was the first one to have a car, so he would drive us to Paris as soon as we could.

DECK D'ARCY: It was a purple Twingo. The style was… *pfft*, but when you are eighteen, you don't care as long as it drives.

CHRISTIAN MAZZALAI: Daft Punk invited us to some of our first parties in Paris.

We discovered electronic music with them. We were sixteen, seventeen. They called us "*les petits.*"

THOMAS MARS: The clubs were horrible. There was no scene, so these '80s clubs were trying to survive by rebranding themselves. It was dirty, but not in an appealing way. I guess the only good thing is that it was everyone together. If you were not into the drug scene, there was nothing to do. But we'd go because we had nothing to do. I remember standing on the staircase at the Queen in between two levels and looking at people for hours, feeling super bored.

PEDRO WINTER: While everybody was into streetwear and sneakers, the Phoenix boys were looking for the perfect leather boots. They were wearing Charles Ingalls shirts while we were all into Supreme.

CHRISTIAN MAZZALAI: I loved the culture of sampling. Electronic music was the key because you could do it at home.

LAURENT BRANCOWITZ: Suddenly you could buy equipment that didn't cost the price of a car and make a semi-professional record.

DECK D'ARCY: Motorbass, Daft Punk, Air—all of those people knew and liked each other but the music was totally different. There have been so many explanations for French touch, but it's maybe that there's no style: the electronic, do-it-yourself thing encompasses everyone.

THOMAS MARS: When I left for Paris, my dad got me an apartment. But he wouldn't give me money. It was strange being totally broke in a very nice apartment on Rue Jacob in Saint-Germain, a fancy neighborhood. We had nothing. At this store down the street, if you bought three sandwiches, they'd give you three more for ten francs, so we went there every day. We would steal toilet paper from them—anything that we could avoid buying.

CHRISTIAN MAZZALAI: The fridge was always empty. We lived on cheap pizza and soup. That's why we went to all the French touch parties, for the free drinks.

CHAG BARATIN: Our parents had a meeting to decide if it was a good idea to let us all live in this apartment. The main reason was that we were studying so it would save time on transportation. I think Thomas quit university maybe two weeks later.

THOMAS MARS: I dropped out after four days. I had nothing in common with these people. I thought self-destruction was a good way to make sure I was making music. And also my parents had money so you have this weird safety net that can keep you from achieving anything. That can be the worst situation: you're just comfortable enough not to have any motivation.

LAURENT BRANCOWITZ: I was studying literature. I got a few diplomas but I knew it would be totally useless. It was more because I liked to read, and it was the only field where you could get away with not going to class. For a short period I was studying German law. I don't know why.

CHRISTIAN MAZZALAI: I was doing economics. Nightmare. I walked out of a lecture on probability. It was like a movie. The teacher was like, "Stay!" But I couldn't. I slammed the door, I quit. For six, maybe ten months, I was only doing music, hoping to get a deal.

DECK D'ARCY: I was the last to quit. I did mathematics for a few years. It wasn't really uninteresting, and I was trying to work in this flat, which was impossible.

JEAN-LOUIS CROQUET: I was driving to Paris and Thomas asked if I could drop him at university. When I dropped him off, I said, "This is not the university, this is a parking lot." He said, "Oh, this is fine." I discovered that they had quit to play music. I was the last one to know. I was happy for them.

MARIE-CHRISTINE VIDAL: As a teacher I didn't like that they quit university, but the other parents believed in the band and their support really helped me.

CHRISTIAN MAZZALAI: We did everything so that music would be our only possibility.

LAURENT BRANCOWITZ: I got certified as a psychopath so I could skip national service.

CHRISTIAN MAZZALAI: We were the last generation that had to do it. You had to go through three days of testing, and they would give you an area of the army to work in for one year. But if you were too crazy, you couldn't do it. There were different levels. P-1, you can do it. P-2, you can do it but you can't have guns.

THOMAS MARS: P-3, you can't do it but you might be called for war. P-4, you're so crazy, you might shoot your own people.

CHRISTIAN MAZZALAI: So our goal was to be P-4. There was one doctor who you would pay to give you medication and a sentence to say in the tests. This army psychiatrist would try to see if you were lying about being crazy. The pressure was very high.

LAURENT BRANCOWITZ: I was P-4? P-3? It puts a bad stain on you! It means you have some psychological disturbance. But back then there was no choice. Doing military service was the ultimate nightmare. I think I would have collapsed. So we were really happy that we found this medic. He cost five hundred francs.

CHRISTIAN MAZZALAI: I didn't do it because at eighteen, I had the option to be

Italian or French. So I am Italian, still. Thomas, Branco, Chag all lied well. Deck is too smart. He's P-2.

DECK D'ARCY: It's the only time I saw a shrink. The others went to a more expensive psychiatrist who does a proper letter. I just had a prescription for anxiety medication. I wasn't a great actor—for context, when we made the video for "Too Young," I had to reshoot my part about twenty-four times, and everyone was crying with laughter because I was so bad—so I had to repeat the test so they could see if I was really crazy. But I never passed it again because then they stopped national service. I think some of us are still considered hardcore defective. It turned out pretty well.

THOMAS MARS: I got P-4. Lying to the military shrink is my best performance to this day.

DECK D'ARCY: Officially there was meant to be four of us living in the apartment: Chag, Chris, Thomas, and me. Branco was living downstairs in a studio flat. But it was never just the four of us, not even for one night. I think the record was fourteen people sharing the beds. There was no privacy.

THOMAS MARS: Our lifestyle was crazy unhealthy. I think I saw the sun rise every single day for eight years. I would go to sleep at 10 a.m. and wake up at 5 p.m. It was years of sedation. Watching strange T.V. at night. Horrible programs that we became cultish about. There was one episode of this fishing show with a famous French artist who loved fishing. Now it seems normal that a guy likes food and music, but at the time it was ridiculous. We would laugh for hours about it. We would wait for it to come on and let out the loudest cheer at 4 a.m.

DECK D'ARCY: It was not a very productive place.

ROB COUDERT: It was somewhere between an artist's squat, a headquarters, and an ashram. The band were always there, brainstorming or playing video games.

THOMAS MARS: No one was cleaning anything. We smoked so much. One guy threw his cigarette in the trash, went to Monoprix, then realized what he'd done and came back to the kitchen on fire. One wall was burnt. It stayed like that.

CHAG BARATIN: Thomas had a sofa-bed. Once he pulled it out and caught a mouse by the tail between the bars. The mouse was trapped, screaming.

CHRISTIAN MAZZALAI: My mother was always complaining about us not being shaved and not being clean enough. We had a crazy friend who never washed his clothes. He took them off, threw them in a pile, and moved it about once a year.

CHAG BARATIN: We were all working different shifts at hotels. You would come home at 8 a. m., and slide into a bed that someone had just left. You could still feel the hot sheets.

NICOLAS GODIN: As long as you didn't sleep there, it was fine. Though if you broke up with a girlfriend, you could crash there any time.

CHRISTIAN MAZZALAI: We had crazy, endless parties. Everyone would come.

LAURENT BRANCOWITZ: This student was living downstairs, working on the preparatory exam for a big school.

DECK D'ARCY: She bought us a massive piece of carpet to put in the kitchen—her flat was underneath—to try and insulate the noise. It was so big, I don't know how she got it up the stairs.

LAURENT BRANCOWITZ: We often think about how we destroyed her life because we were so noisy. Aude Pluvinage, I'm sorry.

THOMAS MARS: Sébastien Tellier threw up everywhere, down the wall of the stairs. Higher than the mouth. Eye level. It must have been projectile. No one cleaned the wall so it dried and it stayed there for a year or something.

SÉBASTIEN TELLIER: They were our crazy years! It seemed like the world was opening to us with a big smile. It was huge luck that we got to experience this

together. It was a flamboyant youth full of promise. We knew the luck we had and we took full advantage.

DECK D'ARCY: I lived in this flat for fifteen years, I think, until 2009. I was the last one to leave.

CHRISTIAN MAZZALAI: The apartment was too small to rehearse. We would go to Versailles in Deck's purple Twingo every day, 2 p.m. until 6 a.m.

THOMAS MARS: We had a demo with four songs. One was a Bob Dylan cover, "Visions of Johanna," to fill space. We met two record companies that had no bands that did anything outside of France. They were friendly but they said, "It has to be in French."

LAURENT BRANCOWITZ: It wasn't a surprise because our vision of the French record industry was that it was evil. It was a desolate place for music. There was nothing we could relate to. There hadn't been for decades.

CHRISTIAN MAZZALAI: After this meeting, we said, "We will never go back to see a record company, they will come to us." We were very inspired by Beck and the Beastie Boys, whose label Grand Royal was very beautiful, modern, a way to escape the rules.

THOMAS MARS: We made five hundred copies of a seven-inch. We thought they would become collectors' items so we signed a few under a sticker that Branco had designed. We loved taking care of every detail. Getting rid of the middle man also felt really good.

CHRISTIAN MAZZALAI: We created the label, Ghettoblaster, and a fake character called Ross, who was actually me. A friend of a friend was working at a label, and they gave us a list of every French radio contact. I would call, put on a deep voice, and pretend I was Ross from South America. I created a lot of fake artists that were supposedly on our label.

PEDRO WINTER: One day I dropped a cassette tape on Philippe Ascoli's desk—Ascoli was head of Source, a sub-label of Virgin France. Home of Air, Mo' Wax, Money Mark, most of the coolest things at that time. The tape was handwritten, with a "Ghettoblaster" sticker on it, introducing the classic Phoenix touch: Italo-Hawaiian F.M. songs and raw garage jams.

CHRISTIAN MAZZALAI: Daft Punk were one of the biggest bands at the time. They did a mainstream radio show and played "Party Time," which got on a few radio stations. The magazine *Magic* had one small page for new releases, and they gave us a full page. They loved it.

DECK D'ARCY: They wrote that we were geniuses, we are the future.

THOMAS MARS: It put you on the tiniest map, and that was enough to start.

MARC TEISSIER DU CROS: The guy who ran *Magic* showed me this full-page piece. It might have been '96, '97. My office called them, and I think Deck was on the phone. He was a bit blasé.

DECK D'ARCY: I was trying to play it cool.

CHRISTIAN MAZZALAI: Deck is the nicest guy when you know him, but he can be very austere. He was very abrupt on the phone. Afterwards we were asking, "Who is it?" "A guy from a record company." "What?! Why are you like this? You should have talked more!" "Yeah, I think he wants to meet us."

DECK D'ARCY: I quit university the day that Marc called. You can't compete with the idea of doing an album, which had been my dream forever. If you find the tiniest pretext to quit university, it's the right time.

MARC TEISSIER DU CROS: I heard this seven-inch. One side was a really slow tune with a woman talking on top of it, excellent. And the B-side was "Party Time," more punk. It was different from anything you would hear then. You could tell they were really open-minded when it came to music.

NICOLAS GODIN: I heard their demo cassette through Marc. For three or four years, French music was all drum machines. When you hear that cassette, it's like the Strokes five years early. As a French person, I never thought making a band was cool because of our culture. But for some reason, they were cool.

JASON SCHWARTZMAN: Brian Reitzell came back from drumming with Air and he had this sampler. He was telling us all about Phoenix, these young guys who have been friends since they were little, who make incredible music and live in Versailles. I thought they lived in the castle, then I realized it was also the name of the town. I think something was said about jogging in high school, so every time I thought of Phoenix, I had no idea what they looked like but I just pictured a track team, flush-faced, shorts, running, French.

PEDRO WINTER: Philippe Ascoli seemed to liked it and asked me to set up a meeting with the band in his office. In my still-new capacity as Daft Punk's right-hand man, I introduced Branco and Chag to Source. My only goal was to make everybody comfortable, dropping a little joke here and there. I'm sure Philippe Ascoli quickly realized he just met one of the coolest bands in the world.

PHILIPPE ASCOLI: I wanted to sign them the minute they came to my office, without listening to anything but the garage-rock track they released on their own label. We talked about our love for the Beach Boys, Serge Gainsbourg, and James Taylor and Carole King.

THOMAS MARS: Branco came back and said, "I think we're going to get a contract." That was the best day. Suddenly everything you did is validated and you at least have a shot. It was hard to go to sleep, it was so exciting.

LAURENT BRANCOWITZ: After the success of Daft Punk and Air, suddenly things felt possible. There was a new generation taking charge in the record companies. Emmanuel de Buretel, the guy who ran Virgin, was very ambitious. He signed Daft Punk. We were thinking about destroying these borders where French music couldn't permeate America and the U.K. We were very arrogant: we knew it would happen, and it did. Even if we came from France and had zero opportunities, we were sure that the world would love us. It was as simple as that.

THOMAS MARS: Source were doing these compilations. You could do the worst demo ever and get on it, you barely had to be able to play.

MARC TEISSIER DU CROS: Every time we had a compilation to prepare, we would ask friends if they had any interesting music. That's how we found basically the the whole of what's now considered French touch.

CHRISTIAN MAZZALAI: Air had exploded from the first compilation, so they wanted to do another. Source wanted us to do something very live as they'd only heard demos like "Party Time." So we did exactly the opposite: our only electronic song, "Heatwave."

THOMAS MARS: It was '98, so we were twenty-two, twenty-three.

LAURENT BRANCOWITZ: It wasn't like we met Source and they said, "We want to sign you." We went to their office a lot and made them listen to our demos.

CHRISTIAN MAZZALAI: We were always going because they had free cigarettes.

CHAG BARATIN: They had an espresso machine. That was the best. You could do as many espressos as you want without paying.

CHRISTIAN MAZZALAI: Marc had a good vision because there was almost nothing there. He could just see we had ideas. So we didn't sign on one song, we just signed hoping we will write a good song.

MARC TEISSIER DU CROS: It was great that there were two brothers in the band—it's like a guarantee that they'll stay together.

LAURENT BRANCOWITZ: One of Marc's friends was an advertising creative. They were doing a commercial for a Swedish chocolate bar. We needed money and they needed a song in the vein of Ennio Morricone, so they asked us. It was the first time we went to a real studio. Marc knew Sébastien Tellier was very good with Morricone vocals. So he came to the studio with two packs of beer and a lot of honey, because in his mind, when you're singing you have to have honey. He got very drunk. He was a very troubled guy back then. We didn't use anything he did. But it was a really good day. This money made us survive for a long time. I think the commercial was aired once. After a few months, Source gave us a contract. We were very paranoid about contracts. It was the period when Prince had "SLAVE" written on his face. This was traumatizing to witness. It fed our paranoia against the mainstream.

LAURENCE MULLER: They were fierce and suspicious, they knew how to protect themselves. I remember their stubborn insistence on having full artistic control. Their contract was like lace; they had supreme power over every detail.

LAURENT BRANCOWITZ: It was for three albums. We were maybe the last ones to benefit from those kinds of contracts. But then very quickly, when we released our first record, the industry collapsed. The amount of money was infinite for late-'90s bands. Maybe that's why the music was so bad.

CHAG BARATIN: Pedro had helped them with Source, and then they said I should become their manager. The only thing I remember is him telling me, "The most important thing is to say no with a smile."

PEDRO WINTER: I gave a bit of my life to Daft Punk, I know Chag did the same with Phoenix. If I showed him a way of doing things it was just to be 100 percent with and for the band. We wrote our own rules.

THOMAS MARS: We didn't worry that we would lose anything in signing. We were with our best friends. We couldn't wait to be everywhere together. It felt like a holiday.

UNITED

2000

Other voices: CHAG BARATIN, manager. STÉPHANE "ALF" BRIAT, *United* co-producer. ROMAN COPPOLA, filmmaker. SOFIA COPPOLA, filmmaker. ROB COUDERT, keyboards. JEAN-LOUIS CROQUET, Thomas's father. NICOLAS GODIN, Air. PIERS MARTIN, *NME*. URSEL MAZZALAI, Christian and Branco's mother. JASON SCHWARTZMAN, actor/musician. MARC TEISSIER DU CROS, Source Records. PHILIPPE ZDAR, *United* mixer/Cassius.

THOMAS MARS: We signed to Source and Marc and Philippe Ascoli said, "Let's put you on tour with Air."

NICOLAS GODIN: The record label told us we had to go on T.V., play showcases. The record was made on the computer, but there were no computers that let you play shows at that time. Source were about to sign Phoenix, so Marc proposed them as our backing band.

MARC TEISSIER DU CROS: We knew they would get along. For Phoenix, it was a good way to learn the ropes.

NICOLAS GODIN: We had this meeting in Marc's office. When a band enters a room, you know it's gonna be good before you hear the music—it's just about the energy, the charisma. When I saw them, I thought, wow, they've never made a record, but you could tell they already had that.

THOMAS MARS: We kind of ruined Air, because Air was this perfectly produced band and we were a punk band backing them. We destroyed their sound. We were wild, loose—I was playing drums, which I was not good at. We did *Top of the Pops*. I think Supergrass were on. Lenny Kravitz. He was on the same label, so we were at the parties with Virgin, which had parties like Spinal Tap had parties.

DECK D'ARCY: We did John Peel.

CHRISTIAN MAZZALAI: And *Jools Holland*.

NICOLAS GODIN: We didn't know about *Top of the Pops* and all these traditions they had in England. It was like landing on another planet. We had no experience at all, them nor us. We didn't have engineers, roadies. We would carry everything ourselves. Before Eurostar, we had to take a boat to cross the Channel—it was a nightmare.

CHRISTIAN MAZZALAI: We met with the record company. The guy was having a cocktail at a bar. He looked at me and said, "You can have one. The record company will pay." It was the pure, simple pleasure of going to crazy hotels and crazy dinners. They were making fun of me for trying every food. It was very fun because we were totally naïve and all the pressure was on Air's side.

NICOLAS GODIN: We would book them four hotel rooms but they would put all the beds in one room. It was very funny.

CHRISTIAN MAZZALAI: For us, sleeping in separate beds was impossible. When there was a big bed, we were sleeping two in the big bed. We wanted to recreate our little flat where we lived with Chag. The same kids, different hotels.

DECK D'ARCY: We had no idea what it was to promote an album. We could see how record companies were a mix of greediness and total extravagance.

CHRISTIAN MAZZALAI: Sometimes we would wear wigs. There was one Victoires de la Musique ceremony where we played with Air, and us four all had very realistic fake moustaches, combed hair, ties, glasses. We wanted to do punk rock mixed with pads, very Bauhaus. I remember playing in front of the minister of culture, who was appalled. It was like a school band show, very amateur. I loved it.

MARC TEISSIER DU CROS: They were unknown so nobody would have recognized them! But they were thinking forwards.

THOMAS MARS: Air had Mike Mills direct a bunch of videos. He visited my parents' house. One day we were playing laser tag in the gardens with Air. He went back and told Sofia.

SOFIA COPPOLA: I was like, who *are* these guys? Growing up in Versailles seemed so mysterious, so romantic, and exotic, from growing up in California. But we all grew up outside of a big city in an isolated, small-town environment where you're left to make your own fun. They seemed to be like that, which I've always been attracted to. I had found an Air record in London, so I asked them to do the music for *The Virgin Suicides*.

THOMAS MARS: Air wanted David Bowie to sing on "Playground Love," so I was the temp on the demo. They knew Bowie liked their band. So they gave me half a verse and I finished the lyrics, and then because it was my words, it felt natural, so they kept it. I don't think they ever asked Bowie. It's possible that he said no and then they kept it.

CHRISTIAN MAZZALAI: When Thomas sang with Air, he used the pseudonym Gordon Tracks. They did a few shows in America during the release of the movie, and he was wearing a wig, creating a character.

THOMAS MARS: I didn't want everybody to talk about this project when we were going to promote our album. I met Sofia backstage at a weird venue called the American Legion Hall in L.A. She was married at the time. Then we went to the Sundance festival where we played one more show—this trip was where I met Roman.

CHRISTIAN MAZZALAI: We stopped playing with Air because we had to do our record. One of our key rules was to never take advantage of the aura of Daft Punk or Air. There were so many people trying to take something from them. That's why we never said at first that Branco had played with Daft Punk.

NICOLAS GODIN: I could tell they were going to move on. I was really happy for them because I really liked them. Because we were this little country for pop music, there was greater solidarity. As French musicians, we were pioneers. There was no competition like Blur and Oasis. I really hoped they would have the success we were having with their own album.

CHRISTIAN MAZZALAI: We had learned a lot from Daft Punk about keeping our artistic freedom, and we saw the success of Air's first album as their backing band. We discovered all the attention and all the dangers. That's why we created our our publishing company. People were offering us money, but we refused. We were obsessed with freedom and having the rights to everything.

DECK D'ARCY: We hated all the music back then, and especially the French music, and then suddenly there was this moment where all the best bands

-----Original Message-----
From: Ghettoblaster [mailto:ghettoblaster@noos.fr]
Sent: 24 October 2001 03:58
To:
Subject: Funkysquaredance

=20
=20
=20
Dear Mr Cash,

We hope this letter finds you well. Being great admirers of your work, =
we
would be very flattered if you would take the time to consider our =
request.=20
=20
We would like you to cover one of our songs, 'Funky Squaredance', which =
we
would include in our next single. You've been a great inspiration to =
the
writing of this song, and we are sure that a simple version with just =
you
and an acoustic guitar would sound soulful and magic.

In any event, we're looking forward to the chance of hearing your next
record sometime soon.

Yours very truly,

Phoenix
Thomas, Deck, Christian & Branco.=20

--=
----

came from Paris and Versailles. We were twenty, they were our friends—it was super motivating.

LAURENT BRANCOWITZ: Our goal was to traumatize the old guard. And not just the mainstream, but the arty people on the fringe. We felt they lived in a world that should collapse. We wanted the record to reflect the music we loved. We wanted to combine things that weren't supposed to go together, to redefine the aesthetics. It was very arrogant. But for us, it was obvious we had to break those rules.

CHRISTIAN MAZZALAI: We would drive in Deck's car from our little flats in Paris to Versailles. There was a lot of procrastination and trying to avoid work. But we had pressure now from our A&R guy.

DECK D'ARCY: We worked from 5 p.m. to 3 a.m. every day. The writing took six months. The pattern became: whatever we just did, now we have to do the total opposite. The first surviving song we wrote after "Party Time" was "Heatwave."

CHRISTIAN MAZZALAI: Source were putting pressure on us to write a single. They wanted something electronic, but the first track we did was "Honeymoon." Everything they asked for, we delivered the opposite. After we wrote "Honeymoon," we didn't want to do this kind of song any more. We got bored and learned. It was naïve discovery. "Too Young" came from a keyboard that adds harmonies so you can create tricky chords with two fingers. The first songs we wrote were classic pop songs, and towards the end, we wanted to surprise ourselves. In the end we had "If I Ever Feel Better" and "Too Young," which were good for Source.

DECK D'ARCY: We thought we were making a punk album in a very not-punk way. The last track, "Definitive Breaks," has a double saxophone solo with reverbs. That was not super hype in '99.

ROB COUDERT: I think the first time I actually played with them was in the studio while recording *United*. They had a clavinet laying there and asked me to play on a few tracks—"Too Young," "If I Ever Feel Better," "School's Rules," "Embuscade." I was very into clavinet at this time, with a J.C. Vannier approach like in Gainsbourg's "Cannabis."

DECK D'ARCY: We kept all of his first takes.

CHRISTIAN MAZZALAI: We had already put saxophone in one song, so we thought, what else can we do? We wanted to write a country song, but sung by a robot. We saw all this fantastic equipment with Air that we wanted to use. We thought the idea had never been done. This song about death. So we had the vocoder, then we had the idea for a crazy electronic part, then we did this hard-rock riff. It was pure experimentation. We wanted it to be very long.

DECK D'ARCY: We knew it was weird but that was the point. The best part comes at seven and a half minutes.

CHRISTIAN MAZZALAI: The idea was to put the best part at the end, so people have to suffer. Thomas always called it the "dark gospel." When he found it, it was a magical moment. We were the masters of the world at 4 a.m. in this little base-ment in Versailles. Thomas was addicted to Coca-Cola. We had run out. Every-thing in Versailles was closed so we had to drive to a gas station near Paris to buy Coke. It was very depressing in a way, but we were the happiest people in the world. By the time we got back, Branco and Deck had mixed it. That's the part we always cherish: when we don't control it and something comes. If we have this once every two years, I'm happy. This was the first time it ever happened.

THOMAS MARS: Me and Branco each wrote half of "Funky Squaredance." He wrote the beginning, "It feels so hard to win, so hard to lose," which is kind of Hank Williams. Then my part starts and it's very cryptic, very strange. I made up the words and because the take was good, we didn't want to change it.

LAURENT BRANCOWITZ: Deck's mom's choir is in the end of "Funky Squaredance." A lot of our friends are in there shouting and clapping—we really wanted to involve everyone we could.

MARC TEISSIER DU CROS: We had to find a big studio. It was basically all the French touch artists being directed by Pedro telling them what to shout and scream, a mythical moment.

JEAN-LOUIS CROQUET: Still today, "Funky Squaredance" is my alarm. Whenever I take pills for my heart, the music reminds me.

ROMAN COPPOLA: I loved how unusual the song was. There's so much diversity, stylistically, and the lyric is very curious. I believe they had like, eighty-five

hundred dollars to make a video, so it was evident we had to do something that could fit that budget. I was laying in bed in London, where I was working, and thinking, "What could this video be? This could be anything." That thought actually ended up in the video itself—it gave birth to the idea of doing it through concepts and ideas portrayed in that scroll format. There was a lot of exchange, which is also told in the story of the video, but when we finally finished it, I wrapped up the video and sent it as a physical package in the mail. It was a real act of love, of super respect and feeling that we were collaborating on something really special.

THOMAS MARS: Roman sent us the video as a Christmas gift, which we couldn't put out because it was all these copyrighted pictures.

CHRISTIAN MAZZALAI: We couldn't believe it, it was fantastic. The best gift. It's in the Museum of Modern Art.

LAURENT BRANCOWITZ: Thomas and I wrote the lyrics for the album together. We wanted to do classic things with a twist. Love songs but with a political vocabulary, things like that.

THOMAS MARS: For me, the lyrics were very visual. For "Honeymoon," I had just watched *Body Double*. "Too Young," maybe that was *The Sure Thing*, a coming-of-age, road-trip movie. I was trying to come up with whatever I could. With Branco, everything was very distilled, very calibrated. I knew I needed to do more because I was not good at this.

LAURENT BRANCOWITZ: Loss of innocence, the passing of childhood—that's one of Thomas's obsessions. It's a very important part of his personality. His fear of losing innocence has always been something that would consume him. It's in a lot of songs and he talks about it a lot. When he lives something, he knows he's never going to relive it. So he keeps this sense of loss, even if it's good. Maybe it was the fact that we were living a life that felt like being on a permanent holiday with your friends. I guess maybe he knew that it would not last forever.

THOMAS MARS: More than that, even. I never read Proust, *À la Recherche du Temps Perdu*. But I read about this emotion in it where the son is waiting for his mother to kiss him goodnight, and that emotion is the best moment of his life. For me it's exactly the same. The best part is the comfort of the anticipation and the most anxiety is towards the end. I once took medication for it, that's how bad it became. It's a weird thing that sometimes keeps me from enjoying life. It's a bummer. I don't know where it comes from.

LAURENT BRANCOWITZ: We did all the demos in Thomas's parents' basement. Then we did the album in a proper studio. We've always been very paranoid about recording studios. They feel very sterile. Maybe it's because we saw pictures of beautiful places from the past, and when we were beginning to do music, it was really different.

MARC TEISSIER DU CROS: It was a nice studio, Gang. We spent money with no hesitation.

THOMAS MARS: You rent fancy studios for two weeks and the pressure is huge, it's not the way we like to do things. Source gave us Alf, who had worked with Air. We agreed because we didn't know anyone else.

DECK D'ARCY: We considered ourselves the George Martins of Phoenix—why do we need another guy? But we didn't know how to produce.

STÉPHANE "ALF" BRIAT: They had high, uncompromising expectations, and slim studio experience. Despite being young, they had quite a lot of beliefs that they wanted to push their collaborators to follow. The challenge was daring and terribly exciting, so I tried everything I could to make it workable. *United* wasn't made in a traditional way for that time. There were a lot of pitfalls—we threw ourselves into a puzzle that had one hundred thousand pieces.

THOMAS MARS: Alf was very friendly but he had total control. From the top, we should have said, "No, we're producers."

DECK D'ARCY: It was always exciting to use equipment and then suddenly you can't really touch things. Maybe I was getting on his nerves because I was too controlling. But when you know what you want, you know what you want.

NICOLAS GODIN: As close as you can be with them, they will never let you in when they're creating.

THOMAS MARS: Everything we wanted to do, we were shut down. Deck had to tie his shoelaces to look at the compression setting because we were not allowed next to the board.

STÉPHANE "ALF" BRIAT: Everyone was constantly asking questions and it was sometimes difficult to provide acceptable solutions for everyone. The production time was getting longer and I was responsible for deadlines. We could feel the fatigue.

THOMAS MARS: I told Marc, "This is not working." I remember Marc witnessing Alf pushing Deck away from the board. It was a relief that he finally understood what was going on.

STÉPHANE "ALF" BRIAT: The delay meant there was no time to rest before mixing. The label rejected my request for a break. So I started mixing without taking a step back. The group wanted more than they knew how to express, and I was slammed. We finished recording the album on our knees, going over every detail. It was a bit like using matches to scale the Château de Versailles.

THOMAS MARS: We said to Alf, "It's not going to work."

CHRISTIAN MAZZALAI: The guy leaves, so we are alone with nothing. The album cost a lot. We had ten days more in this studio to save the situation. So we worked with the assistant, Julien Delfaud.

STÉPHANE "ALF" BRIAT: Having assisted Philippe Zdar before, I offered to hand him over. Knowing his temperament and talent, I thought it might produce a result. Then I went on holiday.

CHRISTIAN MAZZALAI: We called Thomas Bangalter, and he said, "I know one guy, Philippe Zdar."

DECK D'ARCY: We thought Zdar was a dickhead. And he had a bad opinion about us.

PHILIPPE ZDAR: I had met them at this party at Colette. I was in a mood. When I saw them, I thought they were showing off, and they thought I was showing off, too. I think we were both super shy. It was a very short encounter in the corridor.

THOMAS MARS: For France, he was a big shot because his band was successful. Somehow, he was the only option.

PHILIPPE ZDAR: The guy from the record company called. I was not completely sure I wanted to do it because I was not really into "Heatwave," which was an instrumental—it was not so unusual for me, as a D.J. And then Thomas Bangalter came to my house, and from the moment he played me "Too Young" and "If I Ever Feel Better," I knew I wanted to do this album. It was completely fresh. A good pop song was groundbreaking at the time. They were doing something that nobody was doing.

DECK D'ARCY: We got along right away. He's such a character. Even the way he says "hello" is a vibe.

PHILIPPE ZDAR: It was really love at first sight. I wanted to make an impression because they were quite frustrated by their studio experience. Everybody was a bit stressed because on the first day I chose "If I Ever Feel Better" to work on, but I wanted to make a statement: now, we're going to do it very well, very professional, and we're going to start with the big songs like we're very sure of ourselves. And in fact, that made a good impression because the mix was super cool. There had been a lot of fights, but they completely trusted me from day one, which is very important for me.

LAURENT BRANCOWITZ: The first thing he told us was, "Touch the desk, do whatever you want, don't be afraid." He appeared like a Christlike figure. It sealed our friendship forever.

DECK D'ARCY: He's both opinionated and also super open-minded. We were meant to do only five tracks because he was working on something else. But he did almost everything.

LAURENT BRANCOWITZ: There was a total eclipse of the sun. We were in the studio and we all went out for this moment. Suddenly the birds stopped singing. We were in the middle of something very important for us, and this physical coincidence was really magical. It's my strongest memory of this process. My memories are maybe more legendary than real, but I think it was the perfect day.

STÉPHANE "ALF" BRIAT: I wasn't really surprised by the result—it's largely the same as what we made, Zdar had just reinflated the tires and polished the chromes. I think we all lacked experience. Their high expectations were a source of stress for me. It wasn't without pain, but it was obviously formative for us all.

CHRISTIAN MAZZALAI: We only did one show before releasing the album. There was a conference in London with all the Virgin guys from around the world. Air and Daft Punk were there.

DECK D'ARCY: It was at Tokyo Joe's, a sushi restaurant. The people from the record company were eating and talking while they watched us.

PIERS MARTIN: I recall white walls and soft lighting and chi-chi décor—a kind of cocaine hell. I can't say people were falling over themselves to get a ticket.

THOMAS MARS: We played our worst show as our first show. Every magazine, every radio was there.

CHAG BARATIN: One of the worst moments in Phoenix's career.

CHRISTIAN MAZZALAI: We were not ready at all. We had never really played live. We brought a ten-piece band. We just wanted to be different. It was a catastrophe.

PHILIPPE ZDAR: They played so bad. I told Thomas, "Fuck, you're never gonna make it." It was terrible. And to do it in *London*.

PIERS MARTIN: I was fully on Phoenix's side and wanted to support them in the *NME*, where no one else was particularly bothered about them. I wasn't as wowed as I'd wanted to be, but I decided to accentuate the positives. I think I used the phrase "George Michael Jackson" to describe Thomas, which seemed like a good idea at the time.

PHILIPPE ZDAR: It was so bad that everyone knew they had to work like maniacs, and that's what they did. It was a good way of starting in the lion's cage.

CHRISTIAN MAZZALAI: This album had absolutely no compromises. We were a big mess because we wanted to control everything, even the sleeve. The vinyl of *United* is too big—we wanted a very thick, high-quality card sleeve, so it's an inch bigger than most L.P.s. The cost was so high, we lost money even if we sold them.

THOMAS MARS: The day the album came out, my grandmother couldn't find it because one copy had been stocked in each section: One in *musique du monde*, one in pop. Another marketing issue.

LAURENT BRANCOWITZ: When the record is released, it's always very sad because you have the feeling that the world will change forever, people will fall on their knees, the water will part. But the truth is, nothing happened. We don't really care anymore, but back in the day, it was a shock.

MARC TEISSIER DU CROS: We had high expectations. It was a critical success more than a commercial success.

CHRISTIAN MAZZALAI: The reviews were very mixed. It was pretty weird because half of them were very bad. Half were very good. We knew it was better than middling.

THOMAS MARS: Daft Punk, Cassius, and Air were on M.T.V. all the time. We weren't because we were different. People wanted more of the same.

DECK D'ARCY: We were not a proper electronic band like them, so I'm sure that many people hated us without hearing any music.

NICOLAS GODIN: People were fed up with the French touch. It was such bad timing because I really loved the record and I loved Phoenix, and I thought it was so fucking unfair. What I admired is their fighting spirit. They didn't care, they moved on.

PIERS MARTIN: Phoenix were the fourth hip French act in four years to be launched by Source, and perhaps fatigue was setting in, both with those peddling the music and those on the receiving end. Or perhaps Phoenix lacked a bit of edge; the world was not exactly short of pretty indie quartets. The British music press didn't know who to write about or what would sell copies at that time, and Phoenix wouldn't help them shift issues.

PHILIPPE ZDAR: It was not music that people were really waiting for. It was very yacht rock, West Coast. People were into techno and hardcore hip-hop. I think that people who became fans of Phoenix really became fans of Phoenix.

JASON SCHWARTZMAN: I was in a recording studio with my band Phantom Planet. Our singer, Alex Greenwald, walked in with this C.D. It was *United*. Yes! I know them! They're French! They're physically active! So the first time I ever heard Phoenix was through super hi-fi speakers. It was the ultimate experience. The album was like a magic trick or someone cooking an incredible meal: *How did they do that?* It was so singular.

DECK D'ARCY: We kind of liked not to be liked in France.

PHILIPPE ZDAR: There was a little bit of jealousy in France. In rock and roll, people tend to respect only the people who have problems. Phoenix are very kind people from Versailles, the city of kings. Even if you are poor in Versailles, people think you are rich. The jealousy was also, "They are making feel-good music while the world is in trouble."

LAURENT BRANCOWITZ: There was an aspect of aristocratic pleasure in being disliked. But also the profound feeling that beautiful music had the magical property of being undeniable. We thought it would apply to our music and that the sheer pleasure of listening to it would overcome the taboo.

DECK D'ARCY: We were not credible on paper. I remember at one festival in France, half of the crowd was super fans, and half of the crowd hated us—like *physically* hated us, you could feel the hatred. They were shouting, "Go back to Versailles."

LAURENT BRANCOWITZ: We had either hostility or misunderstanding. People liking us for the wrong reasons. Especially in the U.K. where they connected us instantly with soft rock. We hated Steely Dan then. A lot of the time, people praising us were kind of insulting us. That's the way we read it.

CHRISTIAN MAZZALAI: Our goal was that the media could not put a stamp on us,

Hopefull

Rainy days and stormy Night
It feels as hard to win as it's hard too loose
Under the burden of my loneliness

I won't enjoy my collection of stamps
when i'm 5 feet under the ground

Now your chewing gum on my coffin
Take me where i long to be
Don't they dig my grave with some excavator
Use a blood stained sword & of snow white horse
Dont you keep my ashes in a rusty tin can
Let them out, free to be blown away

Lonely streets and dusty roads
Lord it's a long way to go back home
I can't believe that you want me to wear
that evening tails that will suit my corpse

Here i lay on my dying bed

They say ~~that~~ an end can be a start

~~I~~ feel like i've been buried ~~but i'm~~ still alive
Yet

It's ~~the a~~ ~~bad dream~~ that never ends
nightmare

Tellear please that you're sure it will ever stop

12

I ~~feel~~ the ~~chaos~~ ~~all~~ around me

A thing i don't try to deny

I'd better ~~learn~~ to accept that

There are things in my life that i can't control

13

You know i don't want to be clever

to be brilliant or superior

             true like ice like fire

Now i know that a breeze can blow me away

~~Now i know there's~~ much

~~much~~
I can ~~find~~ more dignity

In defeat than in the shiniest victory

~~There's more dignity in defeat anyway~~

I'm losing my balance on ~~a~~ tight rope
            the

~~I keep thinking about the good times with you~~

~~an fighting~~ to persevere my last hopes

so almost no one was getting it. It was pretty chaotic because they thought we were D.J.s because our first song was "Heatwave." They didn't get the idea of these worlds colliding. Also we were lying to the press all the time. We said we had been a Prince cover band, a Hank Williams cover band.

LAURENT BRANCOWITZ: The way we experienced music when we were growing up was completely decontextualized. The only contact we had was with the record and the music. One picture here and there, liner notes. A book about David Bowie was the most you can get. We had never heard his speaking voice. So our relationship with music was very pure. We loved the mystery of the heroism, the legendary stuff. If people tried to know more precise things about us, we felt it would kind of ruin the magic.

DECK D'ARCY: We lied in interviews that session players had made the album. Then everyone was saying, "Phoenix don't even play their own music." It was a private joke that nobody could understand. Typical Phoenix of 2000.

LAURENT BRANCOWITZ: We always joke about fighting to stay semi-professional. We fear the world of professionalism. It would destroy the magic. We were always very careful about preserving the friendship. It was related to our paranoia about seeing the Beatles write diss songs about each other. We felt that might happen to us if we weren't careful.

THOMAS MARS: There is a seriousness to professionalism, a level of ambition that is kind of disgusting. Some sort of absence of poetic feeling. We didn't want our bond to be hurt by any of this world.

LAURENT BRANCOWITZ: We said no to every commercial, every press picture. It was fun for us but I guess a nightmare for other people. But all the people we were working with in France were also discovering these new markets for the first time. It's only when we were working with English or American labels that they really couldn't understand us, whereas in France we were more like pioneers discovering how this should be done. We were lucky we could use that as a way to do very stupid things.

CHRISTIAN MAZZALAI: We had maybe our biggest success in France with "If I Ever Feel Better."

DECK D'ARCY: Our parents felt that we became huge stars when they saw us on T.V. The song was big, not the band. They went from, "You have to go to uni," to, "*My son!*" Showing off to their friends.

URSEL MAZZALAI: I realized they could make a career out of it when I heard "If I Ever Feel Better" on the news on German radio. I turned the volume up very loud and danced with my mother.

CHRISTIAN MAZZALAI: In Italy, we had the biggest radio hit of 2000: every Italian knows "If I Ever Feel Better." After that, nothing. It was a success, but it was a misunderstanding.

THOMAS MARS: We played an Italian T.V. show where they couldn't get the rights for football, so they had a nun watching the game in Rome, the business guy in Milan, then a peasant for a southern club. All the clichés. It was fun but it was a circus. It was not about music. We asked to play live, and they didn't even understand the concept. To make it more fun, we spent the night before the show in our hotel room making fake plaster casts to wear during the performance.

LAURENT BRANCOWITZ: We built the first layer of a kind of cult following.

MARC TEISSIER DU CROS: The first tour wasn't very good. They lacked repertoire. Also they were not really ready. It was a bit amateur; it sounded thinner than what they expected from themselves.

CHAG BARATIN: It's not that we were not a live band. It's that we were a bad live band.

LAURENT BRANCOWITZ: We were very lucky because it was a period where music was very bad, so even when we were terrible, we were one of the best.

THOMAS MARS: We weren't disappointed that we weren't as successful as the other bands. I don't know if we were in denial. There was no master plan anymore.

LAURENT BRANCOWITZ: The learning curve was really long. We knew what we wanted to achieve but it took longer than we expected.

THOMAS MARS: You start with the intention to conquer the world, then it becomes more about taking pleasure in being the four of us in a German city where there's nothing to do. Maybe it was healthy. There was no ego.

DECK D'ARCY: The first shows were in Japan, a big music industry festival in

THE DIRECTORS BUREAU

★ NEW YORK ★ LOS ANGELES ★ LONDON ★

THE DIRECTORS BUREAU

DELIVERY
AP

AUTH. INIT.

NOTE: HANDLE UNDER SECTION 15.B AND 31.B

Sapporo with a very high ratio of hair metal bands. Just being in Japan was already something. Musically it was not amazing, but we were really trying to make something different.

THOMAS MARS: Japan was super refreshing, super brief. But it was already giving us a taste of how to enjoy touring. We were with these other French artists for the first shows. We're in Sapporo and they would go to McDonald's and complain about everything. We wanted to eat all the local food. We'd ask, "So, how was the Big Mac?"—teasing because they were so lame and it was shocking for us. We assumed that they were the exception. But when you tour, everybody's like that.

DECK D'ARCY: It was very enjoyable—bringing friends along on the tour bus, getting to try new food. We felt like sailors. It's really stupid stuff, but when you've never traveled before, it's the best. And at night you're going to play a show in front of people who paid to see you. Even if you're not selling out arenas, it's probably more enjoyable than that. And then we came back to Europe for a proper tour.

LAURENT BRANCOWITZ: Touring was a lot of fun. Our tours were really unprofitable, but it was still a moment when the record industry was rich enough to lose money on artists like us.

ALPHABETICAL

2004

Other voices: ROMAN COPPOLA, filmmaker. SOFIA COPPOLA, filmmaker/Thomas's girlfriend. ROB COUDERT, keyboards. THOMAS HEDLUND, Deportees. TONY HOFFER, co-producer. CÉDRIC PLANCY, stage manager. JASON SCHWARTZMAN, actor/musician. PHILIPPE ZDAR, Cassius.

CHRISTIAN MAZZALAI: We did the last *United* concert, and then the day after, we started *Alphabetical*.

LAURENT BRANCOWITZ: We wanted to work in Thomas's basement again. We got some money from the record company to buy some gear, which we were all really excited about. We were furnishing the space, so we went to Ikea. It was 11 September, 2001. I remember watching the news on the T.V. in the lobby of Ikea.

THOMAS MARS: I called my dad. He was in the mayor of Versailles's office. He told me the mayor didn't believe him.

LAURENT BRANCOWITZ: It felt like we were living this collective nightmare. We heard the second plane on the radio when we drove back from Ikea. That was the first operative day of building this record.

CHRISTIAN MAZZALAI: We wanted to achieve perfection, in a way. That's why it took us so long.

LAURENT BRANCOWITZ: We were obsessed with doing something very modern.

CHRISTIAN MAZZALAI: We were obsessed with having the driest sound. Dry for us means timeless, minimal, something that goes through time.

THOMAS MARS: We hated reverb. Reverb for us was mainstream '80s music.

CHRISTIAN MAZZALAI: We were using a lot of compressors from electronic music in Thomas's very dry, muffled basement. That created the sound of *Alphabetical*.

LAURENT BRANCOWITZ: We were also obsessed by *Voodoo* by D'Angelo. It was hard for us to digest. It reinvented the wheel of musicianship: the rhythm, the modernity of the studio work, the digital possibilities.

ROB COUDERT: The broken beat, twisted synths, Rhodes keyboard, heavy bass.

THOMAS MARS: We always loved when you couldn't tell if it was a drum machine or real drums. That's when we started to play with those hybrid sounds.

LAURENT BRANCOWITZ: D'Angelo also had a very deep culture of good-sounding records. That was important for us, the physicality of good records, something that had been lost for almost two decades. D'Angelo had this modernity, and an unlimited budget.

DECK D'ARCY: We were really lost after we discovered his album. When you're obsessed with something that you don't really know how to master, it's really hard. It took us a long time before we could synthesize this music. It becomes something you want to get close to while keeping your identity.

CHRISTIAN MAZZALAI: For one year, we didn't write one single song. We were traumatized by *Voodoo*.

LAURENT BRANCOWITZ: You can hear that obsession with D'Angelo in this record: a sensation of a groove that's not rock, but more like Marvin Gaye, Prince.

CHRISTIAN MAZZALAI: After one year, we had one song. A ballad, but one with a D'Angelo beat. Very weird song.

DECK D'ARCY: A really boring song.

THOMAS MARS: It was maybe when the four of us were least on the same page. We knew we wanted to try to write a more ambitious, decadent record. We thought it would be nice to have a mellow song. We were never good at working with people, and there was this guy doing all the string arrangements.

CHRISTIAN MAZZALAI: We put almost all the money into hiring an orchestra from the Opéra National de Paris.

THOMAS MARS: We spent all the money in one day. We thought that spending money would get us closer to having something finished. It did the opposite.

CHRISTIAN MAZZALAI: So we recorded it, and we threw it in the garbage.

THOMAS MARS: For me, it was a very sad day. I knew I was resisting and that this song was not going to go anywhere. It's possible that it could have if I hadn't resisted. It's hard to know how much you're responsible. There was no sabotage, but it was on the verge.

CHRISTIAN MAZZALAI: When we decided it was a bad song, that was kind of a liberation. We were depressed. Then one moment, we thought, "Yes, let's destroy it," and we began the album very fast after that. A tiny bit of it became "Love for Granted." It was destroyed but it gave birth to another baby. There's a beauty when you have nothing to lose. The weight is off. And we are still the four of us.

DECK D'ARCY: We started a year of being quite efficient, working in Versailles very late at night and finding things right before we drove back to Paris. Almost every day from spring to fall we saw the sun rise.

CHRISTIAN MAZZALAI: We went to finish the album at Sunset Sound in L.A., a mythical studio where the Beach Boys and the Stones had recorded. We loved the room but we wanted to keep our very not-professional sound.

THOMAS MARS: There were gold records everywhere. That was a bummer. Not because you don't feel you can live up to it, but because the whole atmosphere is so self-conscious, and you want to create your own thing.

DECK D'ARCY: Going to Sunset Sound was a bit of a dream comes true, but I think it's something we probably had to get out of our system. Now we could draw a line between the home studio and the most professional, efficient studio experience in the world. You want a rosewood Telecaster, you call, and you have it in a half an hour. In France, you would need a week to get it, if you can even get it. We were kids, so it was amazing.

THOMAS MARS: We never let the label hear anything. They freaked out because we stayed an extra week or two, which cost a lot.

DECK D'ARCY: We worked from noon to midnight basically every day. We had maybe two days off. We stayed at the Magic Castle motel, which was fun when you've only seen motels in movies and T.V. shows. Gross but cool.

TONY HOFFER: There had been unusually heavy rain, which had caused a lot of crickets to come to the studio. We were mixing to quarter-inch tape, and the room needed to be absolutely silent as any noises would make their way onto the final version of the song.

THOMAS MARS: We were recording "Run Run Run." We listened to the mix and we were like, "What is this in the back?"

TONY HOFFER: We figured out that they would stop chirping if we sent the second engineer, Kevin Dean, out into the live room while we were doing the actual

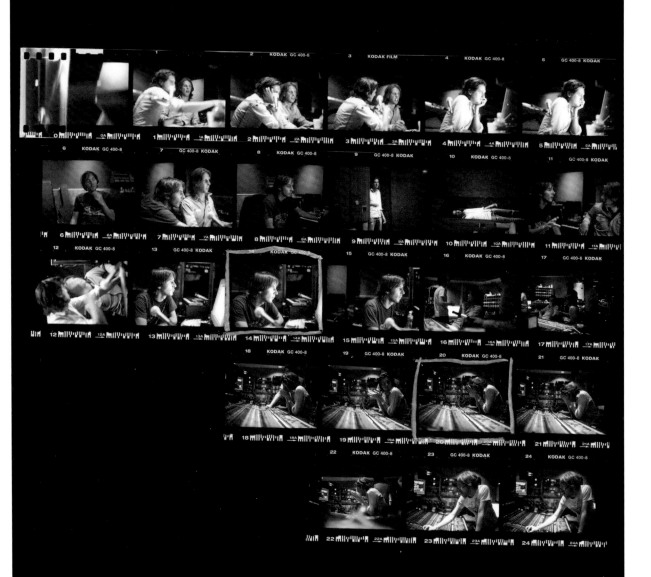

mixdown. Success! The crickets were silent. The next mix was the "vocal up" mix. Kevin went back out into the room and the crickets were silent. But right after we hit record, they started chirping again. They had figured us out and they weren't going to stop.

ROMAN COPPOLA: No one could find this chirping because you can't really perceive which direction the sound is coming from. Everyone's looking for it, and I found this cricket under a mic stand. I was so excited that I was gonna solve the problem that I accidentally squished it. I've been told that it's bad luck to kill a cricket, so I felt badly about that—I didn't wanna bring bad luck on anyone.

THOMAS MARS: We ended up boosting it so much that the cricket sound became the life the song needed.

DECK D'ARCY: Personally, I think *Alphabetical* was the most painful album. Doing ten songs in two and a half years drives you crazy. Now we do ten songs in two and a half years, but we make three thousand pieces of music to make ten songs. We all got sick from nerves. I became claustrophobic and exhausted by working all the time and not finding anything good. We all should have taken some time off, but we just kept trying harder and harder.

PHILIPPE ZDAR: It made me afraid for them because it reminded me of the second album by Cassius, where it took too long and we were putting too much of everything into it.

CHRISTIAN MAZZALAI: Once we finished, we realized very fast that we had created something charming but not perfect at all. Far from it. After this, we discovered the beauty of failure, and of doing something charming that we don't control. We realized that we don't want to have a perfect sound.

THOMAS MARS: The lyrics are so tortured. Cryptic to the point that the song "Alphabetical" is in the past conditional: "If I wasn't that kind I wouldn't care at all." Instead of saying, "I'm done" or "I love you," it takes every back road possible.

It's purposefully immature. I would say it's our least romantic record. "I'm an Actor" was really easy—it's refreshing to talk about fantasies of yourself and get in character. It's a contrast with the lyrics where you're trying to tell people who you are, which took two years. We were so together that we didn't communicate with the world. That level of comfort is huge—you don't have to make an effort with anyone. I just should have been in character more. The record would have been done in three months.

ROMAN COPPOLA: I had a Cadillac Deville, which for some reason had a very vibrant sound system. It was nothing special, just the store-bought system. I would come to visit them at Sunset Sound, then they would do a mix and we would play it in my car. I have to admit, for whatever reason, it was very compatible with their music.

CHRISTIAN MAZZALAI: The rest of us met Roman in L.A. Fantastic guy. We call him Mr. Ideas. We went to his house and he said, "We have to go to the Laundry Bar." It's his bar—you bring your laundry and he makes you a cocktail. "You want to go to the spaceship?" He doesn't explain. "Let's go to the ladder." You go up from his living room and it's like *2001: A Space Odyssey*, all white. "Where do you wanna go, Mars or the Moon?" And a window opens and shows Earth. For us, L.A. was like this—guys like him having poetic ideas.

THOMAS MARS: We went to shoot the "Everything Is Everything" video with Roman. The shoot was on my birthday. At the end, he said, "Okay, see you tomorrow." But I could tell in his smile I was going to see him again that night. He's great at organizing parties, and he had organized one at a restaurant on top of a hill.

ROMAN COPPOLA: It was at the Magic Castle. We saw a magic show.

THOMAS MARS: You had to wear a suit. They rented us the worst tuxedos. Roman sat me next to Sofia. We did prom pictures. I was dressed in the most awkward, the least flattering suit, which I guess was charming somehow.

ROMAN COPPOLA: It's true that I was definitely encouraging Sofia and Thomas to get together. I knew they would be a good fit, so it made me happy to help to connect them.

SOFIA COPPOLA: I loved their song "Too Young." I had it in mind when I was planning *Lost in Translation*. My brother also loved Phoenix, and my cousin, Jason. So when Roman was doing a video for them, he invited me to visit. I have a strong memory of driving around L.A. in Roman's old Cadillac, listening to "Honeymoon" and "I'm an Actor" really loud. I think I fell for Thomas when I heard "Honeymoon." It's a romantic song, and there's something about listening to music when you drive.

THOMAS MARS: When Hedi Slimane came to the studio to shoot the cover, we became aware that after two years of being in the studio, we had to go back out and present the album. It's the longest we've spent between albums—four years since the debut, which is huge.

CHRISTIAN MAZZALAI: We were listening to a lot of hip-hop and Dr. Dre, music very far from us, so we had it mastered by Brian Gardner, who mastered all the big hip-hop records. We were so excited to see him. A very suntanned, old-Hollywood white guy with a toupee. Of course, in the end the album was nothing like D'Angelo. But it's kind of unique.

DECK D'ARCY: We thought people were totally gonna think we ripped him off, but they didn't. At that time, it was impossible for people to think about an indie band using R&B. His music acted like an invisible guide for *Alphabetical* that only we could see in the end.

LAURENT BRANCOWITZ: Even though Napster had changed everything since *United*, we didn't really notice any difference. It was a long process and we never really relied on loads of money. If we wanted to keep control, we understood that we needed to be self-sufficient. What happened for us more concretely is that all the key people we were working with when we signed had changed. Source wasn't a typical record company. They were really music lovers and we respected each other. But gradually all those people moved or got fired. I don't even know which label released us then, it changed so much.

DECK D'ARCY: I think the public struggled to know what we were trying to do, which was probably still the goal. But in the end, we loved this album. It's musical crochet, a U.F.O. In the context of the time, it was quite unusual.

LAURENT BRANCOWITZ: We knew, because it was such a departure, it would be another hard thing for people to understand.

DECK D'ARCY: I don't know if we were really thinking about being big anymore. More about making something different. When you are young, you don't really see the difference between being creative or being big.

THOMAS MARS: We started the tour in Germany. I saw Cédric on the street and he said, "I booked my ticket to follow you with the train and I'm going to see four shows."

CÉDRIC PLANCY: I had been missing them a lot. I had been to a show during the *United* tour. When they released *Alphabetical*, I saw their faces on advertisements everywhere. I became obsessed. It was the beginning of needing to be with them. Because it was our dream to do this music. I wanted to be part of it. I think it had been six or seven years. I was not feeling so good in my job. Finding

them had to be a surprise, I don't know why.

CHAG BARATIN: It was a good surprise. I still don't really know what happened to him during this time.

THOMAS MARS: I was so happy he was back. I said, "You don't need a ticket, come with us on the bus." He came to the four shows. We said, "You have to do something." We hired him to sell the merch.

CÉDRIC PLANCY: It was like we never left each other. I didn't take it seriously at first, but after this German tour, I felt very sad. I knew I needed to keep going, so I got involved in managing the gear.

CHRISTIAN MAZZALAI: We had this crazy success in Norway with "Everything Is Everything." Everyone knew it. Indie fans, customs agents, kids. We were almost more famous there than we were in America on *Wolfgang*.

THOMAS MARS: We toured Norway like it was the United States. We played every small town. We played Oslo five times, enjoying the victory lap. By the end it was embarrassing: people were like, "Okay, we've seen enough of you."

CHRISTIAN MAZZALAI: We were recognized in the street by grandmothers. It was a nightmare. We went on a ferry and school kids of six, seven years old were running after you. We made a rule: when kids recognize you, it's not a healthy sign.

THOMAS MARS: Buying groceries would be an issue. That's the only place where it's happened to me, apart from the day after *S.N.L.* in 2009. There was a late-night T.V. loop where every third song was ours. It was super fun because we were together. Suddenly you experience the city differently. You're walking down the street at 2 a.m. and the guy who owns the best restaurant in town is like, "We're going to open for you. Call your friends, we're going to feast."

DECK D'ARCY: We were lucky to have success in Norway because it's a beautiful country, I had no idea. We felt like demi-gods there. They wanted to please us with anything that we wanted to do. Once, we said we thought it would be fun to fish, and then each time we came back, they thought we were fishermen. They took us fishing everywhere. The cool thing about fishing is everything but fishing—the surrounding, the scenery. You're not meant to kill the fish, but we killed so many fish for nothing just because we were terrible and couldn't release the hook. They took us to the Polar Circle. We went fishing again. The guy takes the fish, chops the head, chops everything, and gets the heart. He puts it down and you see the heart still pumping. He was very proud. We would have probably never witnessed that if we didn't have this radio hit. But we knew from the random success of "If I Ever Feel Better" in Italy that having a radio hit is not something that's going to last very long.

THOMAS MARS: We released a live album from the Scandinavian tour because we were so thrilled with the experience that we wanted to capture the excitement. We wanted to do the opposite of the album, which took four years.

CHRISTIAN MAZZALAI: After that, nothing. That's why we're always looking for balance, because we know success can go. We realized early that the quest for success is a cliché. It's endless. And when you are a success, how do you define it? It's very hard to grab. For us, success was just to release an album.

THOMAS MARS: We met Thomas Hedlund on the *Alphabetical* tour. He was playing with a Swedish band called Deportees.

THOMAS HEDLUND: My bandmates and I had marveled a bit over what we conceived to be their effortless coolness. *Alphabetical* was a really big album in Scandinavia, and I actually practiced to a few of their songs, just out of pure lust. They were super fun to play for a drummer.

CHRISTIAN MAZZALAI: The first time I heard him on this tour was during their soundcheck. He did an Al Green beat with the ultimate feeling just to tune his snare drum. I started a game with Deck to go watch this opening band every night to try to find a single moment of bad-taste drumming. We couldn't believe it: every night, every single second of his playing was perfectly stylish, tight, fantastic.

DECK D'ARCY: He was elegant, handsome, groovy. A hint of cockiness. We had a drummer crush. We had a drummer at the time, Lawrence, and he was good too, especially for *Alphabetical*, but in a different way: he worked well with Chassol, our overqualified keyboard player who was also conducting string orchestras at the time. We asked Hedlund to join after the tour.

THOMAS HEDLUND: I remember being quite starstruck by them, to be honest. We watched their performance at a festival in Sweden and absolutely loved it. It seems that they had a similar experience with me. Luckily, I had no idea at the time. I'm sure I would have been very nervous knowing that they actually checked us out.

THOMAS MARS: Apart from Norway, I never really felt like we were getting more popular. France wasn't into us.

LAURENT BRANCOWITZ: France had changed. What we were doing collectively, no one had ever done. After Daft Punk, suddenly people thought international success was possible for a band from France. Before that, it was that joke about English wine and French rock. We were very conscious about that when we were young and we really wanted to be the first ones to do it. I have really great memories of going to see Sébastien Tellier working on *Politics*. We went to Thomas Bangalter's place in Pigalle one night and listened to *Discovery* for the first time. You're just in your

CUE
SOLO
PATCH
TAPE
CUE
TALKBACK
I'M AN ACTOR
GONG
INTRO
GUITARE
SOUND

friend's room, and it's better than the best music. You didn't know it would change the world but you knew it was the best music you had heard in ten years.

DECK D'ARCY: It was the first time we felt that the contemporary music scene shared our influences. The Strokes were the big ones.

CHRISTIAN MAZZALAI: There's a link with the Strokes and all the French bands: the melancholic, mixed emotions. It's never a perfectly happy song, and it's never sad. It's very French, I would say, but somehow the Strokes have this.

LAURENT BRANCOWITZ: It was a very important rebirth of music. We had a vision of music as a mythical thing, and the Strokes reconnected music with instruments with a strong aesthetic. We felt we were trying to do that with different results. I'm not sure if people saw the connection. They come from a privileged upbringing—I'm not talking about money, but access to culture. They were playing with references that they mastered very well. Whereas coming from a more secluded environment, we had to come up with evolutionary solutions. We felt really lonesome in the world until this wave of bands came.

SOFIA COPPOLA: What I first appreciated, and still appreciate, was their taste. I'm drawn to their aesthetic. Branco is really into graphic design, they're always recommending movies, their references are from all over.

THOMAS MARS: It's strange because when Sofia was shooting *Marie Antoinette*, the production asked my parents to rent their place as the headquarters. We were not together yet. I think it ended up having to be in Paris.

SOFIA COPPOLA: Their house was right next to the garden, so someone asked. It was a coincidence.

THOMAS MARS: *Marie Antoinette* was the first time that Versailles really let someone shoot in the Palais. It was very satisfying because it made it contemporary again. It was the same when there was the Jeff Koons exhibit years later—I'm not a huge Koons fan but it was amazing to see the palace come to life. Recontextualization is huge for us. And that's exactly what Sofia was doing. Marie Antoinette is wearing Converse. There was a Rolls Royce in the palace garden at some point, which I don't think made the final cut. I could really relate. It was like a relief that suddenly something was possible in Versailles.

SOFIA COPPOLA: It was fun for me to know that they used to jog around the gardens of Versailles for gym class. I started to spend more time with them because, by coincidence, I ended up living around the corner from Rue Jacob. Their apartment definitely was like a dorm room or a bachelor pad. It was charming but... a lot of guys sleeping on couches. When we were prepping the movie, Kirsten Dunst, Jason, and I were hanging out together at the club le Baron, which had just opened.

JASON SCHWARTZMAN: I remember walking into this bar and seeing Nicolas from Air. He had his back against one side of this narrow hallway, talking to Chris. *Oh my god, I'm in Paris for no time at all, and that is the man from Phoenix!* Thomas came and sat across from me, and then Chris, and I could tell within three seconds that these were great people. They were just so enthusiastic about everything. I got a feeling that we could be friends.

THOMAS MARS: When Sofia visited me for the first time, she thought it was this romantic Paris apartment. We were bachelors. You would just put the plate in the dishwasher with the food. And we did so much of that, in the end there were a thousand worms in the dishwasher. Maggots. We'd just close it and never deal with it. I don't know how long they stayed in there. It was disgusting. Luckily Sofia didn't open the dishwasher.

SOFIA COPPOLA: That's so gross. I'm not that surprised. It was a lot of young guys without supervision or female influence. I knew there were mice. Thomas would come over to my place, which was much more civilized.

THOMAS MARS: Sofia and I were finally trying to get together. We were at this party and we couldn't get rid of Malcolm McLaren. He was bragging the whole time. I just wanted the guy to leave. It was funny to be hostage of a guy talking about himself, which was the least punk thing. The first time I visited the set of *Marie Antoinette* was the first time I met Sofia's mom. She was making a documentary. For some reason I'm wearing a T-shirt about legalizing weed that Chris Robinson from the Black Crowes gave me, so she thinks I'm a huge stoner. And the whole crew is on an earpiece system where everybody can hear each other talking. I'm with Sofia's mom. This actor in full courtier costume says to Sofia, "So, that is Thomas, is he making great love to you?"

SOFIA COPPOLA: I thought it would be fun to ask them to play the musicians who come to amuse the queen. They were really good sports. They'd have ten-hour sittings with Milena Canonero, the costume designer. I love that they're up for anything. After that, I felt it was like a good luck charm that they had to have a song or somehow be in every movie, since for the first three they had been.

THOMAS MARS: We knew we were going to be dressed like *macarons*. We spent days in fitting for a scene that's a second long. I have tons of pictures of us looking bored in costumes. During a pause on set, we shot a music video with Roman, "Run Run Run," which never came out. And then two weeks later we had to leave for our first American tour—the longest tour we've done, a month and a half. The last thing I wanted to do was go on tour.

SOFIA COPPOLA: I used to listen to "Love for Granted" when I was driving to work on *Marie Antoinette*, missing Thomas.

THOMAS MARS: We landed in Dallas; our first show is in Austin. And I get sick on the plane. I'm sweating, saying, "I can't do this." We arrive and cancel the first show. It was our first show with Rob. I had a spray for cortisone to get better for the second show, and I overdid it. Someone said to take one spray. I took like twenty because I was so nervous. I couldn't sleep.

LAURENT BRANCOWITZ: I have zero recollection of S.X.S.W. I remember we were in the Bush period. Instantly when you crossed the border you could feel the hostility of Republican America. When Trump got elected, I could feel the same weight.

DECK D'ARCY: People were saying that we were allies of Iraq.

THOMAS MARS: Outside our hotel in Austin, there was a car parked with the license plate, "FROG YOU." Some of us got spit on in a bar. In Houston, Chris went to George Bush's bootmaker. He heard the French accent and said, "I'm not selling anything to you guys."

CHRISTIAN MAZZALAI: "Freedom fries." It was real, crazy hostility. The people coming to see us were the opposite.

THOMAS MARS: There was even more of a communion at the shows because of that.

ROB COUDERT: I remember some young people in these towns seriously telling us, "Please, take me with you!"

SOFIA COPPOLA: Thomas showed me pictures from that tour—he's always on the phone, calling me.

DECK D'ARCY: That was so unusual because he was so not like that before.

SOFIA COPPOLA: I would be texting him, and my D.P. would say, "Okay, we have to line up the shot," and it was a really complicated shoot, but I was kind of only halfway doing it because I was thinking about Thomas. I had this poster in my trailer with all the tour dates so I could mark off how long until he would be back. He left at the height of when we were really inseparable.

THOMAS MARS: The time difference didn't make it easier. I think it kind of destroyed her. I would talk to her during the night when she was supposed to rest, so she was exhausted the next day. We were like teenagers. My dad paid my phone bill. He had a family plan. Somehow he never complained.

DECK D'ARCY: Doing a tour in America felt like an achievement. On *United*, we felt like America might be too big for us. This was one of those tours where we felt like everything was history. Not big clubs but cool clubs. Every minute you're in America is so America. We had this sound engineer, Shon Hartman, who loved all the national parks, so every day off, he would plan a visit in odd places in nature. Nature in the U.S. is amazing. He took us rafting in Pennsylvania.

ROB COUDERT: He was a real connoisseur of his country. He took us to legendary Americana sites like Gram Parsons's grave in Joshua Tree, the hotel in Colorado where they shot *The Shining*, beautiful waterfalls, redwoods.

DECK D'ARCY: One night in Ohiopyle, Pennsylvania, we went to this bar to play darts. We talked with guys of fifty, sixty, and they were like, "Wow, you're the first French person I ever talked to. I'm pretty local." Super nice people.

CHRISTIAN MAZZALAI: Our goal since we were kids was to enjoy life and not follow the rock and roll cliché, not stay in the hotel until you go to the concert. I think we are in the top three bands in the world for enjoying life on tour. In America, we had folding bikes and discovered cities.

THOMAS MARS: We had to hire people: one tour manager, one sound engineer, one monitor guy. Chag was tagging along as manager and an extra pair of hands. For the European tours we hired a roadie nicknamed Minimas but we couldn't afford him for the U.S. tour. He came anyway and lived on tiny per diems.

CHRISTIAN MAZZALAI: Our life was crazy, epic, a dream between friends.

SOFIA COPPOLA: They've seen much more of America than I ever have.

ROB COUDERT: I got married in Vegas, another sweet American cliché. It was a lovely midnight ceremony with Chag and Grege, our best friends and then our managers, for witnesses. My wife and I are still married. Phoenix played a beautiful song at the church during the French ceremony we had later.

CHRISTIAN MAZZALAI: It was a big tour, a month and a half, and it was then that we began to discover the danger of touring like an odyssey. We started becoming a good band, but we decided to never tour for that long again. After two weeks you become slightly crazy. You're like a samurai who destroys everything in the city, then the morning after, you're in another city. It's fantastic but there are very dangerous parts.

THOMAS MARS: It was our most extreme tour. The cliché where you drink every night. Because you're twentysomething, you're not exhausted. But when you come home, your body's traumatized. You have a month of recovery.

CHRISTIAN MAZZALAI: As kids, Branco and I saw our uncle playing '60s songs on guitar at dinner. We saw the power, everyone would turn crazy. There were bands in school that formed to attract girls, but not us. We were too weird in the beginning. But then on this tour we discovered the dangerous power of fame.

LAURENT BRANCOWITZ: I've never been attracted to the elements of fame. I think we all avoided it a bit, but maybe me more. I avoid after-parties. I don't really like the unbalanced relationship with people who don't know you. I was more like a monk, reading Borges on the bus. Even when they partied, I was always the last to know what they had been doing. Sometimes they wouldn't even tell me because I was more like a father figure. Even young, I was an old guy.

DECK D'ARCY: Branco didn't go out once, to the point that it was almost suspicious. It wasn't—there was nothing to be suspicious about. I respect that, actually.

LAURENT BRANCOWITZ: I think another two months was proposed. And I said no. It was when we were still trying to figure out how to make this life work. I didn't want to destroy the energy of the band so maybe I said, "Take someone else." Not like splitting, more, "I don't care! Let someone else play my parts for a few shows." I guess it wasn't very realistic.

THOMAS MARS: He said we could go with another guitarist. We could never do that.

DECK D'ARCY: I forgot if we even considered it for one second. It didn't last long. He was the only one with a strong relationship. Six weeks is a long time apart.

LAURENT BRANCOWITZ: They didn't think it was a good idea, but they got the point. It wasn't a big tension. There was this moment where I was the only one mature enough to understand that you have to find the right balance between show business and a life that's worth living. Life on tour can destroy you. Not just because of excess, but because it's a life of perpetually repeating the same cliché. Very fast you become not even Guns N' Roses, because they had some panache, but like the band opening for Guns N' Roses.

IT'S NEVER BEEN
LIKE THAT

2006

Other voices: ROB COUDERT, keyboards. JULIEN DELFAUD, sound engineer. RYAN DOMBAL, Pitchfork. THOMAS HEDLUND, drums. PHILIPPE ZDAR, Cassius.

DECK D'ARCY: Before the end of the *Alphabetical* tour, Chris and I did a recce to Berlin to visit a handful of studios. We had done the '70s Paris studio fantasy, the L.A. fantasy—we had ticked so many teenage dreams, maybe too fast—so we wanted to explore something new. And Berlin was still a bit alternative back then, still exciting. Chris and I saw a few normal studios, and then we visited the Funkhaus. It's the former H.Q. of the D.D.R. communist radio, with all the communist vibes that come with it: totally over-the-top architecture, super austere at the same time. There used to be eight thousand people working there, and by the time we visited, there were only fifty. When the guy who owned the studio received our call to come and visit, he was on his way to close down the company. The equipment was crap, nothing worked, but it didn't matter; we were gonna bring our stuff.

THOMAS MARS: The Funkhaus felt like a very strange, abandoned Versailles palace.

LAURENT BRANCOWITZ: We were looking for a studio that wasn't contaminated by thousands of bands and gold records. We didn't like them. This studio hadn't changed since the '50s or something.

THOMAS MARS: We were already picturing the photo album of our memories. We wanted it to be iconic and we wanted to have a story. What was annoying is every time we said Berlin, everybody would mention Lou Reed, Iggy Pop, Bowie. But we didn't want to go to Hansa or anything that existed before.

CHRISTIAN MAZZALAI: After the last concert, we didn't even go back to Paris; we went directly to the studio in Berlin. We took Julien Delfaud, the engineer who was preparing coffee and assisting on the first album: "Come with us! We're going to make an album very fast."

DECK D'ARCY: We were so excited by doing new music because we spent so long in the studio for *Alphabetical*. I remember two and a half years was like a limit not to cross. When My Bloody Valentine's *Loveless* came out, every article mentioned that it took them two and a half years and that everyone was traumatized. That became the mythical number. After we had reached that point on *Alphabetical*, we felt we had to make the next album quickly.

LAURENT BRANCOWITZ: The first albums, we were kind of under the spell of America's golden years of entertainment. When we did this album we were disconnecting from this influence. We were more into Europe and trying to build something that was ours. We feel that some people are stuck in romanticizing '70s America, like *Phantom of the Paradise*. We felt the richness of Europe, how different French movies were to sleek American movies. We were watching a lot of Truffaut, Italian movies, listening to Krautrock. We got really into Kraftwerk and really thought they were the only band we could relate to—not in terms of their output, but trying to create a kind of mythology of Europe. Continental Europe was strong in the visual arts, but never strong in terms of pop music. Having this goldmine to explore was very exciting.

THOMAS MARS: My mom's German, the brothers' mom is German. *It's Never Been Like That* is like a fantasy version of Germany. I went to Germany as a kid, before the wall came down. My family had escaped the east and now lived in West Germany. The austerity was not appealing. For the brothers, it's more radical because Germany and Italy are the opposites in terms of lifestyle and culture.

LAURENT BRANCOWITZ: When my brother and I were kids, we never liked Germany; we preferred Italy. So it was a rediscovery of those roots and building some new ones.

DECK D'ARCY: From this point we kept on doing this: all of our French, Italian, German influences started gluing to each other.

LAURENT BRANCOWITZ: We never write on tour. So when we stop touring we are filled with this energy, and we always have this naïve illusion that it's going to be very simple to transform this energy into an album. This time, we had to do it because the record company was paying for us to come up with an album.

DECK D'ARCY: We had no songs. We pretended we did to the record company. That was a positive side of being signed to a major. So we locked ourselves in the studio for six weeks.

LAURENT BRANCOWITZ: The whole place was kind of ours. We ate a lot of potato and bacon. It was my last year before I became vegetarian.

CHRISTIAN MAZZALAI: We wanted to do a simple album with simple emotions.

It was liberating to do something very fast.

LAURENT BRANCOWITZ: Thomas was starting a new life, new love. A lot of us had this feeling of freshness. The album is filled with this energy. Especially Thomas, who was like a very sweet fruit about to explode.

CHRISTIAN MAZZALAI: During the last days of recording in Paris, we were working every day until dawn. I never wanted to sleep, I was too excited. We had only one night off. That evening, I met my wife, Julie, in a bar. The next day, I was recording the guitars of "Sometimes in the Fall," which felt like it reflected this feeling—hectic and full of new love.

DECK D'ARCY: With *Alphabetical*, we wanted to disturb people, but it disturbed us more than anyone else. It was like using a nail file to make a marble sculpture. We had many ideas but didn't know how to achieve them. Our reaction was to try to stick to the songs this time. I think it's the only time we achieved what we had in mind before we started an album.

CHRISTIAN MAZZALAI: There was pressure from ourselves to do something better, but we were not looking for perfection.

LAURENT BRANCOWITZ: We had "AUSTERITÉ" in big letters taped on the wall of the studio. That was the keyword.

DECK D'ARCY: It's Julien Delfaud that wrote "AUSTERITÉ." He stayed with us after we stopped working with Alf, before we started with Philippe. We were kids and nobody really knew what they were doing, and there was a lot of emotional drama, so it created a really strong friendship.

JULIEN DELFAUD: They wanted to play live as much as possible. When we added too much post-production and edited too much, we were losing the essence of the songs. Step by step, the album started to look like the building we were in: simple lines, some kind of less-is-more philosophy. We spoke a lot about the albums that John Lennon made with Phil Spector where a simple slapback echo can do a lot more than any reverb. That's when we started to talk about *austerité*.

THOMAS MARS: That's the first album with Thomas Hedlund. It was the first time we had a drummer who had similar taste to us.

THOMAS HEDLUND: They had asked me if I could join them for a tour, but I was already touring the U.S. with my band, the Perishers. So I had to say no, which felt kind of crazy as I was super flattered and excited that they asked. Finally, they reached out again when it was time to record a new album. I was super happy and said yes on the spot. I loved their music and had gotten such a good vibe from them.

DECK D'ARCY: Hedlund was the most important element. It was like rediscovering the way we made music. In Hedlund, we found a perfect combination of style, kindness, creativity, technique. You tell him something once, he remembers. And he's a sweetheart. Everything went very fast with him in place.

THOMAS MARS: There's nothing around the studio except the river. And a gas station, which became a reward. If we'd come up with something we liked, we'd go to the gas station and get food.

LAURENT BRANCOWITZ: Life in Berlin was very poetic. Just the mundane—taking the tram, going to the corner restaurant, having a routine—was very important. It was the discovery of a new set of rules for a good life.

THOMAS MARS: Our apartment was the set of a T.V. cooking show in an office building. There was one bed, like a love bed in a round shape. It turned. There were not enough beds so we would sleep in the hallways. We were not excited to go back there because we knew we would sleep poorly and have nothing to do.

LAURENT BRANCOWITZ: I was sleeping on a very beautiful and very uncomfortable Mies van der Rohe "Barcelona" bench.

DECK D'ARCY: But we were all together and going to the studio every day. We were constantly working and it worked; we did many songs very quickly.

THOMAS HEDLUND: We could be quite honest from the start, and that felt like a testament to our trust in each other. And, since it was the first time we worked together, everything was new and possible. It felt like we were searching for something that was vulnerable, romantic, and almost brutal at the same time. A fun quest, for sure.

THOMAS MARS: I was away from Sofia, and every idea was coming to me pretty quickly because I wanted to get back to her. But I'm enjoying being there too. I think it's one of our most romantic records.

LAURENT BRANCOWITZ: Thomas wrote all the lyrics. I was pushing him to tell the truth. I felt that was very important.

THOMAS MARS: The previous one was so dishonest that it was kind of a necessity. Now there was so much happening in my life that it was easy. But I was always shy—when lyrics become very personal, it's kind of hard because you still want it to be the voice of everyone. Branco freed me from this just by validating the idea.

DECK D'ARCY: The songs are much closer to reality. "Long Distance Call" is pretty straightforward. As a person, Thomas changed so much, it's crazy. When we were working in Versailles on the first album, he would come downstairs for an hour or two, and the rest of the time he was watching T.V. From *It's Never Been Like That*, he became a machine. He was much more positive.

THOMAS MARS: There was a feeling of urgency. When you're locked in a place for two months, you have to come up with something. But also it was time away from these precious things. *Alphabetical* was done in my house, so my bed was right there if I wanted to take a nap. My computer, my T.V., every distraction. Now I had more drive.

JULIEN DELFAUD: We did some overdubs in the basement of Thomas's house. One night we drove back to Paris and I said, "Guys, you have to listen to this"—it was a piece by John Adams, the minimalist composer. They went mad. After that I put a Steve Reich piece, "Music for Eighteen Musicians," and that was a blast for them: the mix of aesthetic and a modern form of composing.

DECK D'ARCY: It took us three months. It was stressful but pretty efficient. We went back to Versailles for a few weeks, then we went to this commercial '90s studio in Paris where depressing, mainstream French artists used to hang out. It was closing down. Randomly, Cassius were the only other band there, so it felt kind of like we had taken control of the French music business Death Star. It was symbolic, in a way, of the new times to come, at least in our minds.

LAURENT BRANCOWITZ: We met at a café on the day we had to hand in the cover. I wanted to call the album *Loyauté*—loyalty. That's the name of our record company. I still think it's a better title, maybe the only regret I have. By the end of the conversation, we had switched to *It's Never Been Like That*. It was feeling like a new beginning, and also it was in the lyrics. I think *Loyauté* felt a bit too serious. And maybe we were in a more teenage exaltation mode. Actually, now I realize it was a good title. I change my mind.

PHILIPPE ZDAR: When I asked them the title, they had to tell me three times. "Wow, it's not good!" If you have to tell the title three times, there's something wrong with it.

LAURENT BRANCOWITZ: We felt that there was a community of music lovers around the world that was very small, but very enthusiastic. We thought it was an album for the *initiés*. But actually, it wasn't.

DECK D'ARCY: We never thought it would become a big hit, but we thought it would connect more with the vibe of the time.

LAURENT BRANCOWITZ: It was in *Rolling Stone*'s end-of-the-year review. We noticed that the reception was suddenly very easy. There was no misunderstanding anymore. People just got it as it was. Maybe our music became easier

to understand. There was some deep love of music that I think we had trouble explaining in the beginning.

RYAN DOMBAL: It placed at No. 13 in Pitchfork's best albums of 2006. It came out at exactly the right time. Phoenix were definitely scratching that effortlessly cool, twin-guitar itch.

DECK D'ARCY: That's the first album where people were shouting the lyrics during the gigs. The tour was really cool because the songs were true to the album. Before, we always had to rearrange the songs because they were impossible to play. It's having Hedlund too. A good band is a good drummer; the rest is filling the gaps.

ROB COUDERT: Hedlund literally brought the energy, the power, the massive sound that made Phoenix a real live band. His playing is extremely impressive in strength and rigor, and creates such a solid basis to play on. Watching him is also a big thing: His strength, his moves, the way he sets up his drum kit, everything makes it a unique show, and somehow he avoids being too demonstrative. We ended up being called "*les frères tempo*."

CHRISTIAN MAZZALAI: Rob is the perfect musical counterpoint to Hedlund. I've never heard either of them play a single note that sounds wrong for our music. Rob has this French, romantic way of playing keyboards and percussion.

LAURENT BRANCOWITZ: Something clicked live and we could feel it was becoming stronger. It had a lot to do with Rob and the Lund.

THOMAS MARS: The tour in France was fun for the first time. They liked the record. The planets were aligned because now there was a scene of young bands. The press was getting excited, like British-style. It collapsed really quickly.

DECK D'ARCY: We could feel that America cared a bit more, but we were not really ready for America yet. We ruined our first Coachella at the beginning of the tour because we had stupid technical issues.

THOMAS HEDLUND: We were so motivated and eager to do a good show, we felt almost like a sports team secluding ourselves to focus and channel energy. Then the day came and we went down to Indio. It was so, so hot but we were stubbornly wearing suit jackets. When we started playing, we almost instantly noticed that Rob's keyboard was malfunctioning, so we had to do some of the more iconic songs without synths, which obviously was a huge downer.

DECK D'ARCY: It was the year that Daft Punk blew everyone out of the water with their pyramid stage, so it was bittersweet.

THOMAS HEDLUND: Over the years we've learned how to deal with those situations. But that first time it felt like a small disaster. We were pretty heartbroken afterwards.

DECK D'ARCY: The failure made us want to be less amateur.

ROB COUDERT: I think after their austere concept in Berlin, they were happy to get rid of the funky fantasy of *Alphabetical*, and they wanted to go back to a rather teenage vision of playing: rock, spontaneous, angrier. We would start the set with "Napoleon Says," and it was obvious from the very first note that the show was different, more in your face. It felt so good to add some wilderness to the music. This is when we started to play the epic jam that ends with Thomas going into the crowd or climbing up the venue.

THOMAS MARS: Sometimes I would have visited the whole venue by the end of the show. I would grab the bartenders and bring them back on stage. People would lift me up to the balcony and I'd get stuck there. I always had a long cable that tied me to the stage like an umbilical cord, which the crowd would hold above their heads. That's how Cédric knows where I am. One night I saw a huge kitchen knife come out of the crowd. Someone cut the cord. I didn't

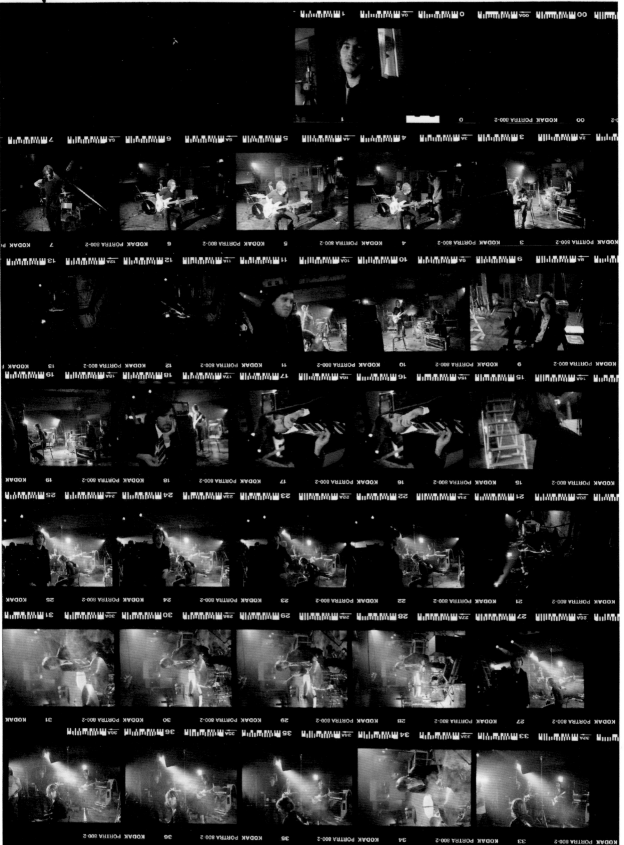

take it as something scary, even if part of me was thinking, "Who *does* that?" More like, "You're staying with us."

LAURENT BRANCOWITZ: Every step was always a victory for us. We were really lucky that we could enjoy them all. People who have more instant success get everything at the same time, the positive and negative, and never can really sort out what happened to them. We had the time to build our defenses, to know what's good about life, and enjoy every little success. Not a big sugar rush, more savoring. Every time the crowds were a bit bigger without losing the previous ones.

THOMAS MARS: I had a party for my thirtieth birthday on 21 November, then 28 November my daughter was born, and on 30 November, we played l'Olympia. It was the end of the tour. A relief that everything went well.

DECK D'ARCY: We were growing up. We were all turning thirty. I don't remember that being a particularly scary prospect. We had Hedlund, we had Rob, we had a great band together. We felt like we had something to build from.

PHOENIX

IT'S NEVER BEEN LIKE THAT

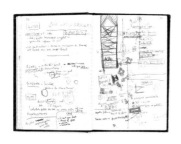

WOLFGANG AMADEUS PHOENIX

2009

Other voices: CHAG BARATIN, business, production, and tour manager. ROMAN COPPOLA, filmmaker. SOFIA COPPOLA, filmmaker. ROB COUDERT, keys. RYAN DOMBAL, Pitchfork. DANIEL GLASS, Glassnote Records. THOMAS HEDLUND, drums. CÉDRIC PLANCY, stage manager. JASON SCHWARTZMAN, actor/musician. SÉBASTIEN TELLIER, musician. MATT WEST, front of house sound engineer. SIMON WHITE, manager. PHILIPPE ZDAR, mixer and producer.

LAURENT BRANCOWITZ: For our first record, there were so many gatekeepers that reaching people was almost impossible. Now that internet culture was gelling, we knew that a kid in Oklahoma City or Berlin could be your soul brother. We thought, let's please this little population.

DECK D'ARCY: We were meant to do a fourth album with Virgin but discovered we could drop it. They wanted to sign us again but we were not happy. They always let us do what we wanted but they never really understood the band. Maybe we didn't really give the keys to be understood.

THOMAS MARS: I felt they thought we were cool to have on their roster, but no one was really pushing us. We wanted to be a priority.

DECK D'ARCY: We did the album ourselves with our money and waited until the end of the process to find a label.

LAURENT BRANCOWITZ: We didn't have a studio. We noticed that people who became successful suddenly buy a place, turn it into a studio, and lose some kind of vital energy. So we have always resisted that. But it makes our life a bit more complicated because we don't know where to go when we start working on a new album.

THOMAS MARS: I had moved to New York in 2008. Somehow our most successful records came after I moved. If it had been the opposite, we would have started doubting ourselves. It showed us that it's possible.

CHRISTIAN MAZZALAI: We had this fantasy of living in a hotel to write: to know the receptionist, to be part of the world. One of our idols, François Truffaut, used to write in the Beverly Hills hotel, or in Japan. So we began to experiment in New York at the Bowery Hotel. We were there three months. For the first time, we put a big table in the room: to talk, to work out everything, to start to experiment. Since then, we have always used this technique.

DECK D'ARCY: We liked the conference table vibe. We felt more like *Wall Street Journal* editors having a meeting than a band jamming.

CHRISTIAN MAZZALAI: We never really liked jamming because it can lead to automatism, where you are doing stuff you control.

DECK D'ARCY: We didn't do much there. Part of "Rome." It was not a very Truffaut experience in the end.

CHRISTIAN MAZZALAI: After New York, we wanted to keep this flow. So we rented a flat in Paris for a month: the atelier that belonged to Géricault, a very famous French painter. Again, we used a big table.

DECK D'ARCY: We were more productive there. We did one of the parts of "Love Like a Sunset." There were massive windows facing north so you always have the same light: you don't really feel if you're in the morning, evening, or midday. It's a very strange atmosphere. We stayed there for two weeks.

CHRISTIAN MAZZALAI: Then we rented a houseboat on the Seine, in front of the Eiffel tower. That was a disaster. We were seasick! We tried for one month but we couldn't do any music.

LAURENT BRANCOWITZ: Being seasick is not the most inspiring feeling.

DECK D'ARCY: I loved the boat but I was the only the one. I actually ended up living on it because I found it so cool—I had been living in Branco's old flat on Rue Jacob.

CHRISTIAN MAZZALAI: Then we went to Philippe Zdar's studio. We hadn't worked with him since *United*. But every album, there was always a moment when Philippe was giving us advice. His studio was under construction because there had been a flood.

THOMAS MARS: It was a soundproofed space but that was it.

PHILIPPE ZDAR: It was in Montmartre. It was a fantastic place from the '70s, done by an American guy very professionally, but then for thirty years it had gone downhill.

DECK D'ARCY: When we were twenty or so, Thomas and I had our very first studio experience in this studio, at the end of its original existence. We were helping Air. Thomas played drums and I played bass.

PHILIPPE ZDAR: I bought it in '99. And then I broke everything so that I couldn't work until I redid it. It took a lot of guts to destroy. The first day, I took an enormous hammer and broke the toilets. I cut all the cables. I didn't destroy the beautiful things, but what I suppose was the last fifteen years of people not taking care of it. I knew if I started working in the place as it was, I would regret it because I would continue working. I was used to going to New York to work with rappers, and I would always fantasize about American studios. I wanted it to be beautiful, like my home. It took a long time. I was doing the refurbishing part by part, weekend by weekend, because I was busy D.J.ing. Everything I earned, I spent. It was like this for seven years.

DECK D'ARCY: It had to become alive again. And Zdar was the perfect guy to do it. He made every single detail from the light switch to the little wire to plug your phone state of the art.

PHILIPPE ZDAR: Sébastien Tellier did his third album here when it was really a ruin.

SÉBASTIEN TELLIER: I recorded *Politics* alone in a huge room with two small lamps. And when the album was finished, the ceiling collapsed on my material. The place was a bomb site!

CHRISTIAN MAZZALAI: We managed to mix one song there, and then we said, "We love the vibe. Can we stay?"

PHILIPPE ZDAR: They didn't want a studio, just a big room where they could take their time. I rented it to them for a very limited budget.

CHRISTIAN MAZZALAI: We were supposed to stay one month. But we stayed one-and-a-half years.

LAURENT BRANCOWITZ: Some basic construction had been done. But the walls were covered in asbestos. There were technical elements everywhere and a lot of dust. It was on the verge of being unsafe. But for us it was great because we felt we could stay forever. There was no pressure.

PHILIPPE ZDAR: We had to call a plumber to put the toilets back.

DECK D'ARCY: There was no power, no A.C., so we couldn't breathe in there. We had to bring our own fan with a twenty-five meter pipe. We never really cared about comfort—actually, we were almost trying to avoid comfort. We didn't find nice studios very inspiring. Berlin was very austere but much more creative, so maybe we were trying to repeat this.

PHILIPPE ZDAR: I wasn't supposed to work on the album. I was just going to the studio every Thursday and Friday to pick up vinyl to D.J., so sometimes they asked what I thought.

THOMAS MARS: He was already producing in a way. It was pretty obvious that he wanted to do it. Every time he came, it would speed up things because he's so positive.

PHILIPPE ZDAR: We went for a coffee and they said, "*Voilá*, we never had a producer in our life, but we wanted to ask if you would like to produce the album with us." I was very moved. For me it was super good news. When I heard "Lisztomania" and "1901," I thought, I cannot *not* do this record.

DECK D'ARCY: Zdar is a combination of super abstract, poetic, chaotic advice that's really not concrete, then sometimes he's super precise. We really trusted him even if we didn't always agree.

PHILIPPE ZDAR: We don't talk too much about music when we talk about music. We talk about flowers or Francis Bacon or food. They totally understand if I say, "We should do something like a bucatini carbonara, the pancetta should be like *this*."

DECK D'ARCY: I love when he challenges us. "This is crap!" He could almost have tears in his eyes if he doesn't like something, or if he likes something. Sometimes you wonder who's the artist and who's the producer. But that's part of his mystique.

THOMAS MARS: He has an opinion about every single thing in his life. Nothing's left to chance. It has to have a personal touch.

CHRISTIAN MAZZALAI: I asked him, "What's the best pepper?" He said, "Of course! It's black malabar! You cannot use anything else."

LAURENT BRANCOWITZ: Then we would switch to tomatoes.

DECK D'ARCY: He had an American-sized fridge full of champagne. That's his character. A record with Philippe, it's a journey. Even lunch with Philippe is a journey. Five minutes with him is a journey, so imagine a record.

THOMAS MARS: His life seems exhausting. I've never seen a guy who talks to his bank that many times a day.

CHRISTIAN MAZZALAI: Just before we met him, before *United*, he had kidney cancer. After this, he knew that he only has one life.

PHILIPPE ZDAR: I lost my dad when I was ten. He took me to school, and he said, "I'm coming back to pick you up," and then he never did. It was very hard and it made me understand the lightness and the fragility of existence, how everything can go bad in a minute. When it happens to you when you're ten, it's really deep inside of you. And then at twenty-six, I got cancer. But I survived. I was very lucky. Ever since I am young, I want to have the best day possible. If I earn money, I will buy something with it. I think Henry Miller, or one of those guys, once said, "I use my talent for my writing and my genius for my living." This has always worked for me. My living is the most important. I spend a lot of time with my family. If I feel that I need to go away for fifteen days and it's very important for a record, then I do it. If people don't understand, I don't work with them.

THOMAS MARS: Did you ever see Sinatra in the studio? He comes with his girlfriend, his mistress, and his friends, and he's going to sing and impress them, and then they go to dinner? That's Philippe. He needs people in the room.

LAURENT BRANCOWITZ: We talked a lot about trying to grab this teenage emotion where you feel invincible. The nickname we gave it was "*j'arrête tout*," "I quit!" It's Chris's moment from where he quit university and decided to jump in the void of trying to be a musician. It was a very cliché moment! But "*j'arrête tout*" is this exact moment of exaltation.

CHRISTIAN MAZZALAI: We elaborated a technique for writing. I once watched a documentary about Ferran Adrià, this big Spanish chef, and I was shocked because he worked in exactly the same way as us. Six months a year, he would experiment with new dishes. He would take a mushroom, olive oil, cook the mushroom at fifty degrees, and then seventy, then one hundred. Then give stars. No crazy judging. And then he put them on the wall, and came back later. That's exactly what we were doing. We bought many of these cheap

Dictaphone recorders in Berlin. There's a button, "voice up," which we used a lot because it created compression. Our technique was to record everything, and then re-record it with this button. Two weeks later—not before—I listened to everything. Just me. And then I would name the files, put it on iTunes, list the tempo. Then we would all listen three weeks after, then put stars on, categorize it, and put all the parts in. That's how we did *Wolfgang Amadeus Phoenix* and *Bankrupt!*. Very long process, but that's why those songs are like roller coasters.

ROMAN COPPOLA: I visited them at the studio. What was interesting to me was that the music was just budding. It felt very incomplete. I thought, "Wow, how are they gonna turn this into songs?" It was all these fractured pieces, little glimpses. It was very interesting to see it being born.

LAURENT BRANCOWITZ: Chris's role as the archivist, the gold-digger, emerged during these years. He has a very good ear and he can listen to dozens of hours of garbage and extract a little molecule.

CHRISTIAN MAZZALAI: Like the album before, every take was the first take. When you do a second, the charm is finished. Not losing the *jeune homme*, the charm, is key.

LAURENT BRANCOWITZ: Philippe was always talking about modernity. We wanted it to be straightforward—we didn't want to blur another communication.

THOMAS MARS: It took a lot of time to shape. Just before we left for a South American tour, Deck played a motif on the piano and "Lisztomania" came together.

DECK D'ARCY: It sounded catchy but, *pfft*, you never know. We were not teenagers anymore, we had to wait a bit before getting excited.

THOMAS MARS: Chris had the tape, and he was listening on the airplane, like, "That's good."

CHRISTIAN MAZZALAI: The chorus to "Lisztomania" was originally four times shorter. So there was no stability. Philippe had the idea to repeat it. He was so right.

THOMAS MARS: Sometimes if something is very efficient it feels disgusting, so you back away from it.

LAURENT BRANCOWITZ: Our father was very sick. The album has a kind of intensity that's related to that, sadness mixed with hope. Our life was like that. It wasn't like a Hollywood movie, it was more like a French movie.

CHRISTIAN MAZZALAI: Rob's wife is called Maria. She has a very specific, very

hectic dance, so at the beginning of "Lisztomania," we knew we needed more Maria. We called that beat *la danse de Maria.*

LAURENT BRANCOWITZ: It took us a long time to understand that the cheapest guitar had something unique that was more important than something great. This idea changed how we approached our work. The first period, we had to define our own vision of good taste. And then we had to destroy it and find something new.

CHRISTIAN MAZZALAI: We bought many Fender Bullet Stratocasters on eBay. We've tried so many other guitars, but on *Wolfgang,* it's only this very cheap guitar. We had tiny keyboards from the '80s, but fantastic because there's a little mic where you can sample your voice. The cheap digital synthesizer can't handle it; it creates a humanity.

THOMAS MARS: "1901" has kind of a submarine pulse in the beginning, which was a toy instrument. It was like a great perfume that has one percent of something disgusting. I thought we needed this. Philippe was great at validating that.

CHRISTIAN MAZZALAI: During the end of *It's Never Been Like That,* Julien Delfaud drove us from Versailles to Paris and made us discover Steve Reich. It was a big revelation. We decided to do our own soundtrack for this tunnel from Versailles to Paris. We had a Yamaha CS-80, the old-school Ferrari of synthesizers from the late '70s. If you move one button, you never find the sound again. A cleaner accidentally pushed a button. We were like, "*No!*" Deck tried the new sound and instantly found the intro of "Love Like a Sunset," recorded it, and it was exactly what we were looking for. That's what we love, things that don't come from our brains: pure luck.

LAURENT BRANCOWITZ: I learned Morse code as a way to generate ideas that didn't just come from us. You can create rhythms with words. My cat had just died, so I put in a little farewell message to him. I never told the other guys.

PHILIPPE ZDAR: Suddenly I went to Ibiza because I needed it. I listened to the demos in my car. In France it was super pouring rain. I called them and said, "We have to put this album out for summer, it's an obligation." It worked so well in the sun. I came back and we finished the album. Without that moment, we could have spent three, four, five more months on it. And if this album wasn't out for summer, it wouldn't have had the same success.

THOMAS MARS: The lyrics are cryptic because sometimes you write to figure out what you have to say. That's the record that's the most like this. It was pretty much the unconscious making sense without me piloting. I wish it happened more often. The first lines of "Lisztomania"—"Romantic, not disgusting yet"—summed up what I wanted to say. "1901" was about the things I enjoy in Paris that I missed from living in New York. I didn't realize that the theme was reappropriation until later.

CHRISTIAN MAZZALAI: We really didn't want to talk about America. We wanted to talk about European things. It was almost virgin territory in pop, to talk about Franz Liszt instead of the bayou or Highway 61.

PHILIPPE ZDAR: They wanted me to mix it, and they said, "Why don't you finish building the mixing room?" I didn't have enough money to do that. So they paid me nearly one year upfront so that I could finish it. It was very class.

LAURENT BRANCOWITZ: The working title in my head was *Tits and Ass* because it's the most stupid, horrible title. We were discovering the creative power of stupidity.

THOMAS MARS: The title came from a few things. The book *Mozart in the Jungle*. I saw the film *Lisztomania* after I started dating Sofia.

SOFIA COPPOLA: Ken Russell took all these liberties that were very pop: paparazzi cameras, ice-cream sundaes. I wanted to have that kind of freedom with *Marie Antoinette*.

THOMAS MARS: There was a terrible movie called *Liberté, Égalité, Choucroute*, which is a weird twist on the French revolution—disrespectful but making it contemporary. Making things contemporary—that's when I thought, *Wolfgang Amadeus Phoenix*.

LAURENT BRANCOWITZ: Our mom hated it. I swear she cried. She always had the feeling we were shooting ourselves in the foot. We loved it.

CHRISTIAN MAZZALAI: We were very excited because we thought we had something. A lot of record labels didn't like it.

DECK D'ARCY: "Ah *oui*, '1901,' it's a good album track. 'Lisztomania,' I'm not sure."

F   B

3
3
3
3

Acres	1 2 3 4 5 6 7 8
Visible horizon	0 1 2 - 4 5 6 7 8 9
Right where it starts it ends	3 - 5 6 7 8 - 9
Oh when did we start the end ?	0 1 2 3 - 4 5 6 - 7 8

Acres	0 1 2 3 4+ 5 6 7 8
Visible illusion	0 1 2 3 4 5 6 7 8 9+
Oh where it starts it ends	2 3 4 5 6+ 7+ 8+9
Love like a sunset	2 3 4 5+ 6 7 - 8+

Acres	4
Honor is a legion	4
What a disguise we're in	4 X
What a disguise we're in	4

Acres
Invisible horizon
This is where it starts and ends
Love like a sunset

5
6 det 7

CHRISTIAN MAZZALAI: Even our friends said it was a bit too complex.

THOMAS MARS: Jason Schwartzman was in town. He came to listen. It was the best listening party we ever did. He noticed every detail.

JASON SCHWARTZMAN: It was one of the best moments of my life. Pigalle, France. A rainy afternoon. I had now known them for a long time, but going to the studio was another level. You know when you love something and it happens again and it's totally new and you go, *fuck yes!* and everything just comes into focus? *Holy smokes. "1901," oh my god! This is nothing like you guys but it is you guys and nothing like anyone else! Holy shit, the key just changed.* I wondered what it was like to make something like this.

THOMAS MARS: After that we felt ready to play it to some managers. We had met Simon at a festival in Spain. He said he'd always liked us and was super friendly.

SIMON WHITE: I had loved them from the first moment I heard "Too Young," when I was working on a stall in Camden Market. After I moved into management, I was always searching MySpace for artists who sounded like Phoenix. I regarded them as my favorite band. I'd always wondered why they weren't the biggest band in the world. It just seemed like they hadn't been marketed correctly. When I heard via their agent that they were looking for management, I jumped at the chance.

THOMAS MARS: He came with his business partner, Chris Gentry. We played "Lisztomania," and as soon as the chorus started they looked at each other like, "Okay!"

SIMON WHITE: It was a huge step up and seemed to crystalize everything they'd done previously. I presumed the entire music industry would feel the same and instantly embrace them. As it was, that didn't quite happen immediately.

THOMAS MARS: I would go see big indie labels and nothing felt right. I met

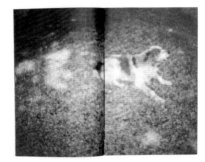
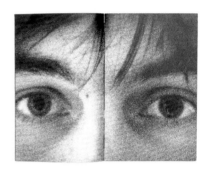

people I could relate to, but in the end the boss would not go for it because we were already kind of old.

SIMON WHITE: Initially no one was interested in signing them. XL, Columbia, Polydor, Warner, Atlantic all either passed or said it wasn't right for them. A lot of people seemed hung up on the fact they were four albums in and hadn't been really successful. One label said "1901" was "cute" but a band in their thirties that had already released three albums was a difficult prospect.

DECK D'ARCY: Vincent Clery-Melin was running an indie label called Cooperative. He had worked in international at Virgin, so we knew him pretty well. He was very interested but we were used to the luxury of a major label, and his label was tiny. Anyway, he was the only person who wanted us, so we signed for Europe with him, but we still had no deal in America.

SIMON WHITE: We really only met Daniel Glass by accident. Alan Becker, the head of Sony Red Distribution, collared me when I was in their office. He was a big fan of Phoenix and had heard that I was managing them. I played him "1901" and "Lisztomania" and he immediately got Daniel on speakerphone to tell him to sign them. Daniel wasn't totally familiar, but when he heard they were French, he put their French intern on the phone and asked if she was a fan. She loved them.

DANIEL GLASS: I only knew of Phoenix as a "cool" band from France. I really did not know a lot about them. As soon as I received the phone call, I went downtown to listen to two songs, which turn out to be "Lisztomania" and "1901." They had a sound I had never heard before. I knew they would cut through at radio and create a new path. I could barely contain myself and I took the subway back to the office to play the songs for our team. I actually left the office so they could listen without me coloring their opinion. I came back about thirty minutes later and they all begged me, "Sign this immediately."

THOMAS MARS: Then Daniel called on a conference call: "We're going to get a gold record, we're going to finish at Madison Square Garden!" We were really impressed.

DANIEL GLASS: This was one of the funniest and most meaningful calls of my career. We called Thomas and it was quite late at night in France. Ten minutes into the call, which we were conducting in French, he said, "You know I speak perfect English?" It was the beginning of a spectacular relationship.

THOMAS MARS: In the next few days he flew to Paris.

DANIEL GLASS: I sat in front of these four cool, thin guys. It was an intense interview. I didn't get up to go to the bathroom even though I had to because I didn't want to break the focus. The conversation lasted a few hours and at the end we summarized the band wanted two things: they wanted to headline a U.S. festival, and they wanted to play *Saturday Night Live*. As far as I knew, the only French artist to ever perform on the show was the Gipsy Kings.

LAURENT BRANCOWITZ: It was the first time in our life we met a guy from a record company who we thought was dreaming far too much. He asked us, "How many records do you want to sell?" We never think in those terms. Simon said, "Maybe fifty thousand?" And Daniel Glass was shocked—too low. "You're crazy."

THOMAS MARS: That was the opposite of anything that happened to us, so, no matter what, we were going with this guy because we were clearly a priority.

LAURENT BRANCOWITZ: After years of being really paranoid about losing control, or being crushed by the mainstream, we were in a lighter mood to try things. We felt our music was stronger. So we enjoyed the cliché of the record company guy from a '60s movie.

CHRISTIAN MAZZALAI: For the first time, we owned the masters—we licensed it to Glassnote—so we could do exactly what we wanted. Releasing on the Internet was not the thing to do then, but giving "1901" away created something crazy.

THOMAS MARS: We wanted people to hear it. "1901" was a gift from the record that had just been done.

LAURENT BRANCOWITZ: We were very surprised by the reaction.

CHRISTIAN MAZZALAI: There was a thing called Hype Machine. "1901" was No. 1 on everything. Zdar said, "This never happened to me since MC Solaar in the '90s!"

DECK D'ARCY: When I received the email about *Saturday Night Live*, I didn't even open it. I thought it was spam.

DANIEL GLASS: I was in Miami Beach with my family and we ran into Marci Klein, the producer of S.N.L. She invited us over to her father's house that evening for drinks and we met her boyfriend. They were both massive fans of Phoenix. I sent them two songs. About a week later, we were home on a Saturday night and the phone rang at 11 p.m. It was Marci and her team inviting Phoenix to play S.N.L. in April. Since this was February, I assumed she meant April 2010. When she said, "No, I mean in six weeks," I gulped, counted to five, and said, "They will be there."

THOMAS MARS: When Daniel called, I was in Belize with Chag on holiday. He called: "We have S.N.L., do you have visas? We need to get visas." It's America so you pay, like, $40,000.

DANIEL GLASS: I had no idea how to do this so we hired immigration attorneys to help us get work visas. It was a challenge. At one point, there was an outstanding parking ticket in France that was holding things up. It went down to the wire.

CHRISTIAN MAZZALAI: Everyone was like, "Why this little band from France?" We were a secret in America. We knew it was a big deal, especially Thomas— he's fascinated by standup, so S.N.L. is like his dream.

LAURENT BRANCOWITZ: Being French, S.N.L. is just a name. So we went knowing it was a big deal, but not being over-impressed. I had no idea who these comedians were. And that's always a great feeling, when you don't know exactly what's happening.

ROB COUDERT: It's probably the first time we faced American show business straight in the eyes. We realized how serious those guys are when it comes to not being serious.

DECK D'ARCY: To be honest, we were not really ready. We were very on edge, beta-testing in front of ten million Americans. It's probably not super smart to do that.

LAURENT BRANCOWITZ: It was a moment where we were technically able to do exactly the live show we wanted. The technology was mature enough that we could sample all our sounds and kind of have our own studio on stage. But this was advanced equipment that was very new and very unstable.

CHRISTIAN MAZZALAI: It's not like a normal T.V. show because you rehearse for four days with the team. On Saturday, at 8 p.m., everyone does a full live rehearsal with the crowd, and then they edit the parts that don't work. It's very old school. We do the dress rehearsal. We are French, so when we do a rehearsal, we don't give everything. We don't pretend. It was working well, we go back to the dressing room.

DANIEL GLASS: The producer Lorne Michaels comes to see me in the dressing room and asks, "What's wrong?"

THOMAS MARS: The last time Daniel Glass had been there was with Sinead O'Connor ripping a picture of the Pope, so he was kind of traumatized.

CHRISTIAN MAZZALAI: Daniel says to us, "That's not the band I signed."

ROB COUDERT: It felt like a mindfuck. We were obviously being manipulated, but we had no clue about their methods.

THOMAS MARS: Daniel brings the producer. They're like, "Guys, do you want some wine?" They wanted us to loosen up.

CHRISTIAN MAZZALAI: They were all freaked out that we would do a bad performance. Americans play for the camera, they pretend. And we were kind of austere. Someone went to buy wine for us. "You like wine, you're French!" And then a guy says, "The producer wants you to play two songs at the end of the show." And we didn't know how to play the other songs because we did not have time in rehearsal, but no one can refuse. So we had to create sounds in half an hour with this tense vibe. The host was Seth Rogen. He seemed stressed too, but he was totally high.

THOMAS MARS: Then when it's the real performance, we see Cédric freak out. "There's nothing." The computer controlling the keyboard midi sounds doesn't work. We were about to be on live T.V. If it doesn't work, no sound comes out of half the instruments.

CHRISTIAN MAZZALAI: We go on stage, "Ten! Nine! Eight!" "Not working!" "Seven!" "Not working!" "Six!" "Not working!" "Three, two, one—" "*WORKING!*" Really like in a movie.

THOMAS HEDLUND: Then the stage manager pointed at me and we started the song.

CÉDRIC PLANCY: We did the best show ever.

JASON SCHWARTZMAN: I was looking around the room like, these people are getting their minds blown right now.

THOMAS MARS: I walk out and high-five Jason. And then the fun is over because Marci Klein and Daniel Glass come back. They wanted us to play another song over the end credits, so four in total. Marci's boyfriend's favorite song was "If I Ever Feel Better," so she asks if we can play it. We hadn't played any other songs for like, four years. So we said no. They said, "What about 'Too Young?'" To get out of it, I said we need a Roland JX-3P with the controller, which is hard to find. Because it's New York City, it's there ten minutes later.

DANIEL GLASS: They had the graphics department write out the lyrics to "Too Young" just in case.

THOMAS MARS: And then we play, and it's really bad, but it's the end credits and we don't care. People are still on their high from the two first songs.

CÉDRIC PLANCY: I watched it on T.V. after and I cried. We did it.

THOMAS MARS: The day after, I had to fly to San Francisco. People at the airport were freaking out, which I've never had before.

RYAN DOMBAL: In the context of the indie rock critical darlings of 2009— Animal Collective, Dirty Projectors, Grizzly Bear—*Wolfgang* sounds so much more direct and extroverted. This was when the blurred wooziness of chill-wave was taking off too. Phoenix felt like a straight-to-the-gut antidote to that.

LAURENT BRANCOWITZ: It was a good period for music. There was an interest for things that were a bit more complicated, a bit less obvious.

CHRISTIAN MAZZALAI: We felt lucky because success can be fantastic but it can be the most horrible thing when it's a misunderstanding; it's always a misunderstanding, but it can be the most horrible thing when it doesn't reflect who you are at all.

LAURENT BRANCOWITZ: Sometimes you are David Bowie and "Let's Dance" makes you huge. And it's not the song that's transmitting his Bowieness in its purest form. For us it was the opposite.

THOMAS MARS: After we did S.N.L., we started a tour in Europe and no one really cared. But I would get calls from Daniel saying we were added to some American radio station that I didn't know. We were enjoying having a crowd

BUS CALL BOSTON 11.30PM

TO DAY ROOM FOR SHOWERS THEN OFF TO NEW YORK

BOSTON TO NEW YORK 5 HOURS

PARK UP OUTSIDE LETTERMAN, BUS STAYS TILL 4PM

8AM ADAM AND MINIMAS TO MTV WITH EQUIPMENT

7.30AM LOAD IN MTV

8AM CEDRIC, JOAKIM, MATT LOAD IN LETTERMAN

8.30AM BAND ARRIVE MTV/MINIMAS AND ADAM TO LETTERMAN

9-9.30AM LINE/SOUND/CAMERA CHECK

9.30-10.15AM PROMO INTERVIEW "THE 5"

10.15 BAND TO DAY ROOM FOR SHOWERS. JENNA WILL ACCOMPANY

11AM-12PM LINE CHECK LETTERMAN

11.20AM BAND RETURN TO MTV

12PM CREW TO DAY ROOM FOR SHOWERS

12-1PM PHOENIX ACO 1901 (GO GET EM FELLAS)

1.15PM BAND TO HOTEL FROM MTV AND LUNCH

2PM CREW RETURN TO LETTERMAN

2.45PM BAND CALL LETTERMAN

3-4PM SOUND CHECK AND CAMERA REHEARSALS LETTERMAN

4PM BUS WITH ADAM, MINIMAS AND JOAKIM TO WILLIAMSBURG

4.30-5.30PM THE LATE SHOW

5.25PM PHOENIX (MAKE IT HAPPEN BOYS)

5.45PM REMAINING BANMD AND CREW TO WILLIAMSBURG

6PM LOAD IN WILLIAMSBURG (BUS TO SECAUCUS)

7PM REST OF US ARRIVE WILLIAMSBURG (TOGETHER ATLAST)

7.20PM PROMO INTERVIEW "FADER"

7.30PM SOUNDCHECK

10PM DOORS

11-1130PM LIGHT SPEED

12AM PHOENIX (LET'S SHOW THEM HOW TO DO IT)

2AM LOAD OUT AND RETURN TO HOTEL (BUS TO TERMINAL 5 WHERE IT WILL STAY TILL WE LEAVE SATURDAY NIGHT)

AND REST!!!

WELL DONE EVERYONE. ABSOLUTELY AMAZING DAY...

that didn't care because we knew it was building in America.

CHRISTIAN MAZZALAI: Our first U.S. show was Bonnaroo. The tent was fully packed one hour before. And then Thomas was late.

THOMAS MARS: I was with Simon in the airport and our flight was delayed. We were almost about to cancel. Somehow, we arrived at the festival ten minutes before the show. I heard the crowd super loud and thought, we can't follow the band before. Then I realized they were waiting for us.

CHRISTIAN MAZZALAI: We did a very bad show but the people were crazy. We were totally new for them, but we were ready because we had played so many shows.

MATT WEST: Two weeks later, we were in Denver at the Bluebird. News came through in the afternoon of Michael Jackson's passing. After the show I decided to switch our outro track to "Rock With You." I figured the guys wouldn't be too disapproving. To my surprise, the whole place erupted into an impromptu M.J. dance party. The band came out to dance with everyone.

CHRISTIAN MAZZALAI: People said, "Keep going!" The owner was very cool, he kept it open. We were crying and dancing with people, one thousand people dancing for hours to M.J.

DECK D'ARCY: When we started the tour, I was single. I was like, I don't need a flat. Between tours I would not come home, I would stay and visit where we played. I did my backpacking years during the *Wolfgang* tour. I chucked everything else, I just had a one-square-meter storage unit in Paris. I'm glad it didn't last fifteen years but it was exciting.

CHRISTIAN MAZZALAI: Deck doesn't care about physical things to an extent that it's almost frightening.

THOMAS MARS: It was so much work because everybody wants a piece of the album. And so we said yes to everything because everything was exotic. We did the strangest meet-and-greets in Kansas. We were the first European people they'd ever seen. "What is that accent?"

CHRISTIAN MAZZALAI: We discovered you had to go around every radio station shaking hands. We felt like American politicians. We never took it seriously. Sometimes we were playing in front of sixty-year-olds. Sometimes it was quarterbacks: "*Huhh, yeahhh, PHOENIX!*" We knew nothing is for granted, so we were cherishing it.

NICOLAS GODIN: They gave hope to any fucking band in France that they could make it in the States. They really opened the door.

SOFIA COPPOLA: Before *Wolfgang*, when people would ask, "What does your boyfriend do?" and I'm like, "He's in a French rock band," people would look at me, like, "Oh... you're dating a guy in a *French rock band*," like, *how pathetic*. Then it changed and people didn't feel sorry for me. That was a big difference.

RYAN DOMBAL: *Wolfgang* came out during the first months of the Obama administration, and the album captures this wide-eyed optimism of the time. If you dig deep into the album, there are a lot of knotty issues of the heart, but on the surface it really seems to glide along without friction. It feels naïve now, but the album was released when a lot of Americans felt this true, pure sense of hope for what was to come. In that way, it clicked.

DECK D'ARCY: Our success has been quite progressive, even if *Wolfgang* was a big step, for sure. We had had little hits here and there, maybe not as massively significant, but those stages helped us handle these situations, the traps you can easily slip into.

THOMAS MARS: It's fun because you're all together, but at some point, you look at the crowd and you're like, this is weird. And then when the hit fades away, the frat boys go away. It's pretty crazy how quickly they go.

SOFIA COPPOLA: It's pretty amazing that someone gets that much attention and success and doesn't lose their minds. Usually you go crazy for at least a second then calm down, but they never turned into nightmares, as far as I could tell.

THOMAS MARS: We were extremely amateur about it. It's hard to get away from the stiffness of how some things were really expected to be, how professional and unlike how we function. I think there was sometimes confusion that we were not comfortable with that position.

LAURENT BRANCOWITZ: Chris and I were living in very dark times personally because our father was sick. So we didn't really care about the outside world. We were happy to travel the world, play bigger shows, and have audiences know the lyrics. It put a lot of perspective into our lives. We were wise enough not to get captured by the whirlwind.

THOMAS HEDLUND: I went through a lot of hardships personally, with my mother being ill and eventually passing away during the tour.

THOMAS MARS: Hedlund got a call saying, "If you want to come say goodbye, you have to come now." And so he had to go. We were in Chicago about to play an arena show for a radio station, at the height of the frenzy around the album. We somehow tried to play a song, just acoustically, the four of us in a giant arena. We apologized but some people booed. It was really weird, a strange feeling.

Telefunken 46db

GIRLFRIEND

16 → 17,
btn minch

73: two...
74: ch.chot

Tired out, not a miracle in days
Deciders for the lonely - whispering tears
You try out for nothing then you drop dead,
Not a miracle in years
Leisure for the lonely whispering unecessary unless you're in
ancien (demo)
it oath or glory   Die for succeed
I say it out loud but she just don't care
Farewell, til you know me well
Farewell, til yell, know me well
Girlfriend
des des des
We are far from home, I am with you now
I am longing you, I am longing us two
Who bought a miracle sells these fortune tears
December's death or glory how you want it ?
Longing for a miracle in here years
Leisure for the lonely wishing death wishes death unless
deciders   lonely ?
Death or glory   Die or Succeed
I say it out loud but she just don't care
Farewell, til you know me well
Farewell, til you know me well
Girlfriend
die & succeed
Sold inhibition but she just don't care
Farewell
die

des des des   .. tears

25 Girlfriend

THOMAS HEDLUND: I truly feared that I would lose the joy of playing, an emotional space that had been so important for me since I was a child, when I needed that space more than ever. But I found it wasn't the case. It's a testament to the power of art and creating something with people you love.

CHRISTIAN MAZZALAI: We realized it was very big when they even recognized us in immigration. We could do anything. We had the keys to the city. If you said, "I love the Museum of Natural History," there was always a guy who knows a guy who works there who would open at night for you. So we went and he opened the backstage and showed us all the animals in formaldehyde. "This is a monkey from 1910." It was so shocking.

LAURENT BRANCOWITZ: A lot of doors opened but the ones we chose to open were those kinds of things. Maybe Axl Rose would have chosen a different option. For me, one of the strongest images in cinema is in *Indiana Jones* when he finds the Ark of the Covenant. At the end, it's put in a crate, and you see a guy from the government put it in the warehouse with thousands of crates. It's forgotten. For me, the dream is to open all those crates. And sometimes it's possible through music.

THOMAS MARS: Everything becomes theater. "Lisztomania" is about the idea of being a spectator of something strange that you can't relate to. It alienates you, but it can be in a good way.

CHRISTIAN MAZZALAI: We played a fraternity house at Vanderbilt University. There were kids showing us beer pong. We didn't know anything! Everyone on drugs, drunk, sleeping, half-dead, at the same time very naïve and crazy decadent.

THOMAS MARS: It was the era of remixes, which we hated. It was the record company trying to say, "You could be on this radio station, or you could be played in the club if you have an uptempo version of this song, so can we contact this person?" In France, we didn't grow up with this idea that you have to ask permission to use your music—you can use an entire song without permission on any T.V. show, as long as it's not a commercial. I think I had the idea that we had to give the stems away. Not only is everybody going to be so happy that they have thousands of remixes, but you assume that the best ones will surface. We liked the idea of being sampled.

LAURENT BRANCOWITZ: Maybe it's Deck's influence, but we love to clean the warehouse. This is a metaphor for our minds and all the ideas we accumulate. When we know that people are going to sample all the beats, take the snare drum sound, it's not ours anymore and we're free to start afresh.

THOMAS MARS: We would hear the stems in original songs here and there. There was a Swedish band, Royal Concept. My sister Anna called me and said, "You put out a new song? You didn't tell me."

LAURENT BRANCOWITZ: McDonald's did a commercial with a fake "Lisztomania." They took the exact same sounds and put them in a different order. It's a problem when your sound becomes public property—somehow it becomes less mysterious.

THOMAS MARS: The only ad we said yes to was Cadillac, because it was so ridiculous. And it was a lot of money. We needed our touring life to be normal because we felt like we would lose it otherwise. For us Cadillac wasn't selling out. When we were growing up, Gainsbourg did commercials, Salvador Dalí did Lanvin. So we saw it as this really pop thing, which few bands understood. It was divisive, which was interesting—you felt like you were playing with stuff that was kind of controversial.

LAURENT BRANCOWITZ: Shakira, or maybe her label, contacted us. Which I found the most creative idea in a way. Imagining what we could do made us laugh.

PHILIPPE ZDAR: One day I received a phone call from my hero, Adam Yauch. He said, "Do you want to work with us? My daughter and I have listened to *Wolfgang* two hundred times and we still love it. It's full of air, like hip-hop." He completely understood what I was doing with this album—a rock, pop album with hip-hop foundations. This album was so important for me because it made me work with the Beastie Boys. And Cat Power. It was really a lucky charm.

CHRISTIAN MAZZALAI: Coachella was one of the craziest shows we've done.

ROMAN COPPOLA: There was this big surge when Beyoncé and Jay-Z were striding up to hang out side of stage. They had some kind of charisma and walked right up without anyone stopping them. That showed the thrill that this was the place to be and the thing to see.

CHRISTIAN MAZZALAI: We couldn't believe there was Beyoncé here, singing all the lyrics to "Girlfriend." "Beyoncé knows the lyrics?!"

THOMAS MARS: She knew stuff that Chris doesn't know.

LAURENT BRANCOWITZ: Being very short-sighted, I of course didn't notice.

THOMAS MARS: Coachella said we could headline next time because we had the biggest crowd.

LAURENT BRANCOWITZ: This period was very complicated in our personal lives because a lot of people died around us, so for me all these memories of this album being very successful are also linked with some very complicated times of pure sadness. My cat died, and then our father died, and our grandmother. Our father had a long period of sickness. I don't know how it's possible, but he passed away between tours.

DECK D'ARCY: The day after the funeral, we flew to New York for a show. Their mom wanted them to go. They assumed that their dad would have wanted it, which I'm sure he would have—he was the sweetest guy. But they didn't want to take a break. It's probably a way to heal, to keep on.

LAURENT BRANCOWITZ: In my memory, it was then that we learned we were nominated for the Grammys. When there's very good news, I always expect the bad news, the weird contrast that makes life interesting. But this part wasn't good, it was too intense.

THOMAS MARS: We had a show at Hammerstein Ballroom in New York when the Grammy nominations were announced. We didn't care, but because everybody around us was excited, it started getting closer. We grew up hating these things. It was something we couldn't relate to, but it felt exotic.

CHRISTIAN MAZZALAI: We could feel that the Grammys was a bit cheesy, but we loved it. There are two shows. One during the day because they don't have time to show it all on T.V. We were on that one. You have a little buffet. We were after like, best polka record. Then we were invited to the real Grammys.

THOMAS MARS: It's really cold and not that exciting, maybe because it's made for T.V. I was sitting behind Slash, so I couldn't see anything. Big hat.

SOFIA COPPOLA: I was pretty pregnant. I remember eating a hot dog at the Grammys stadium because I was so desperate.

THOMAS MARS: There are legends there, but you can't really relate to them because you don't want to admit to yourself that you could be on the same level. We were sitting behind a band that had jackets that said "Party City," L.M.F.A.O. I thought, *I don't want to have anything to do with this.*

CHRISTIAN MAZZALAI: Then we went to the Beverly Hills hotel.

THOMAS MARS: Daniel Glass brings Neil Young. He says, "Neil, they just won." Neil had just won his first Grammy for music. He's like, "Well, it took me forty-five years."

LAURENT BRANCOWITZ: They sent the Grammy to your home. When my brother unpacked it, he told me that he had an instant depression. Chris was the first to see this side of reality.

CHRISTIAN MAZZALAI: I put it in my living room and the next morning, I woke up and felt a bit of anxiety. I couldn't explain it. At night, when I came back, I saw it again. So I gave it to my mother. I think what you get and what you want are two different things. I was very happy to have this Grammy, of course. But I started to see the stress of having a medal. It was what we don't like when we see a gold record in the studio—something that should be very far from creativity.

DECK D'ARCY: It felt good—even if we always found awards a bit incestuous, alternative album was the best category to be in. The trophy is on my mom's piano. I don't want those things in my house. I'm not really into things, anyway.

THOMAS MARS: It could have gone either way: you get addicted to this kind of thing and you want more. But I felt relieved: it felt like a reward, and then you didn't need to chase more of them.

CHRISTIAN MAZZALAI: I needed to get rid of the past to move on.

PHILIPPE ZDAR: One day I was in Electric Lady recording the Beastie Boys. And Phoenix called me and said, "Tonight we're doing Madison Square Garden with Thomas and Guy-Man from Daft Punk," who are my old brothers. So we left the studio early.

THOMAS MARS: Guy-Man and Thomas had come backstage when we played Hollywood Bowl a few weeks earlier.

LAURENT BRANCOWITZ: After the Hollywood Bowl show, we were drinking a glass of sake. In this moment of euphoria, I guess we were excited about the idea of playing on stage together.

THOMAS MARS: And Madison Square Garden was coming. We tried to keep it a secret during rehearsals. I don't know how Daniel kept it together.

DECK D'ARCY: Being able to keep it a secret was the biggest surprise for us—there were already social networks.

WOLFGANG AMADEUS PHOENIX

Phoenix

CHAG BARATIN: Even backstage, we didn't have their names on any signs.

DANIEL GLASS: My wife was able to get a babysitter for one of Daft Punk's children, so thanks to Deborah we got them there.

LAURENT BRANCOWITZ: For me, it had a special meaning because it was kind of a reunion. I hadn't played with them since Darlin'.

DECK D'ARCY: I was excited about the music. We started it over email: a mashup of all the iconic vocoder parts from Daft Punk songs on an extended version of "If I Ever Feel Better" mixed with "1901." Then we went to a tiny rehearsal studio in New York the day before the show. It worked fantastically.

THOMAS MARS: We built their arrival in mysteriously. You hear the sounds, you're wondering, *is this… it sounds like… could it be…* and then it is. Creating that sense of mystery and fear at the same time, something threatening so you're not in a comfort zone.

CHAG BARATIN: It's one of my top five emotional moments of all time. The audience exploded, but beyond the craziness, there was total osmosis between the bands. Madison Square Garden wasn't a big arena any more, it felt like a small club. We ran over the curfew and it cost us fifty percent of the fee. The unions in New York do not kid around.

PHILIPPE ZDAR: Then we were in the dressing room and there was a surprise— the album had gone gold.

LAURENT BRANCOWITZ: After the show, we were driving through the night and there was a big noise. The bus hit a deer. This is the thing I remember the most about this night.

PHILIPPE ZDAR: I took my gold record in the cab. I realized, I come from a very little city in the Alps, I lost my father, and then I was in New York City working with the Beastie Boys, holding my gold record. I went back to my hotel alone. I had too much emotion. So I gave the gold record to the guy at the hotel, and I went out and I had three whiskey sours alone in a bar like an old alcoholic. I couldn't imagine this kind of adventure. This is *Wolfgang*, that's how far a record can take you.

JASON SCHWARTZMAN: A while after the tour ended, Sofia and Thomas got married. The image I remember the most is that the guys in the band were always together at the wedding. They had just been on tour together for years, and they're all huddled over there in a corner, talking and laughing like best friends. You know when you see people who have been married for fifty, sixty years, the way they look at each other? It's like that.

BANKRUPT!

2013

Other voices: CHAG BARATIN, business, production, and tour manager. PETER J. BRANDT, documentarian. PHILIPPE ZDAR, mixer and co-producer.

LAURENT BRANCOWITZ: After *Wolfgang*, I was a bit more cynical about the world. We had seen the big circus, the nightmare, of corporate America. For us the experience was very funny because we were always the same gang of people. But after a while, it destroys a bit of your soul. You have to rebel against it. I remember being in a studio and it was so cold because they have this obsession about being stronger than nature, like creating golf courses in the desert. It was a perfect metaphor for America as we saw it at this pre-Trump stage. Everything was already in place for the big nightmare. It was the beginning of Instagram culture: pure vanity with zero shame.

THOMAS MARS: We knew what we were getting into. It's not like we were surprised by the fact that we were getting more cynical.

DECK D'ARCY: We knew we had reached a different audience that was not necessarily our hardcore audience.

THOMAS MARS: What's unpleasant about the attention is that you become familiar. You lose some sense of poetry and weirdness. And unless you do something totally differently next time, the next thing is not going to be awkward anymore. It's just going to fit. We always go back to a form of expressing ourselves that's awkward.

DECK D'ARCY: The week after we came back from the *Wolfgang* tour, we found a studio and started working. It had been two years since we had done anything new, so we were super impatient to start.

LAURENT BRANCOWITZ: I got shingles, which you get when you're really tired or really depressed.

CHRISTIAN MAZZALAI: I had a weird pain near my heart. I saw like, ten doctors about it. It was linked to stress, anguish. I was not in a sad place; it was more something I didn't control. We didn't think of taking a break, because when we find something together, that's why we are living. So it's very hard to stop. We never thought to take a break, actually. Maybe we should have.

LAURENT BRANCOWITZ: We knew people would listen to this record. On the previous albums, we weren't sure it would happen. So we thought it was our duty to make a record that was a bit more demanding.

CHRISTIAN MAZZALAI: We still believed in our little motto: if it's good for us, it might be good for somebody. It's impossible to guess what people will like.

THOMAS MARS: I joked in the beginning that we couldn't do *Ludwig von Phoenix*.

LAURENT BRANCOWITZ: I know a lot of people who perfect one thing and achieve some kind of perfection that I'm sometimes jealous of. Whereas when we know how to do something, we are immediately bored. I think we are still children watching a magic trick when we are supposed to be the magician. But we want to be amazed by it.

CHRISTIAN MAZZALAI: What we wanted to learn was songwriting. We did a tour with the Pixies in Australia, and we were all shocked at how good they were, the perfection of some of the writing.

THOMAS MARS: We made our most successful record when I was living in New York. But it was the opposite on *Bankrupt!*, it didn't work as well. I was not there at key moments. I missed maybe a week setting up in Paris, which was essential to create the relationship with Zdar and with the owner of the new studio, to establish what people expected from each other.

DECK D'ARCY: Zdar became a big guy suddenly so we couldn't afford his studio anymore. I'm joking but it's sort of true. He renovated it while we were doing *Wolfgang* and it became a really beautiful, fancy, proper studio. We couldn't stay there for two years. We had to go somewhere more intimate.

THOMAS MARS: Chris called me and he was really excited because he said they found a place, Tranquille le Chat, that was in the middle of Paris and had light, which is hard to find.

DECK D'ARCY: We did two or three weeks at T.L.C., trying to find what we are always looking for, a perfect combination of organic and synthesized color. We did some sound research, some palette-building. Maybe too much because eventually *Bankrupt!* became a super-produced album.

CHRISTIAN MAZZALAI: Then we were looking for a place in New York. Adam Yauch offered us his studio for nothing in exchange. It was purely genuine.

THOMAS MARS: He said, "Come for as long as you want." We came for two or three months.

DECK D'ARCY: The studio was in the office of his movie production company. It had been designed for the Beastie Boys—they were the only people who worked there, so it was immaculate. Everyone there was super nice. It matched our desire to always work in unconventional studios.

CHRISTIAN MAZZALAI: He was passing by every day from five minutes to two or three hours. We had very long conversations. He told me so many crazy stories about New York when they began. We told him about Ghettoblaster, and how important him and Beck were for us. I was happy to tell him how important they were for many French musicians. A fantastic character.

LAURENT BRANCOWITZ: Meeting Adam was really one of the coolest encounters. He was really sweet and really intelligent. He was already sick, so we could see that he was kind of struggling. It made it even more poignant.

DECK D'ARCY: We had tea every day. He was doing a mix of green tea and soba, part of the gentle detox for his disease. You could feel he was going to the essential with the stuff he was saying. We weren't playing him anything, it was too early and I guess we felt a bit shy.

LAURENT BRANCOWITZ: I'm not sure what we really created there, but it was a really intense period. It's the time of Fukushima, the Japanese tsunami. We had friends fleeing California because they were afraid of the nuclear cloud. And the French politician Dominique Strauss-Kahn was arrested in New York for rape. It was just happening across the street from where we were. People thought he would be the next French president, and suddenly he got caught in a huge sex scandal. Very weird memories.

DECK D'ARCY: We went back to Paris, to T.L.C., and we sat there for almost two years.

THOMAS MARS: Laurent d'Herbécourt, who owned the studio, liked our music and wanted to be involved in making this record. He didn't know how slow we are. We need little input. And I think he got frustrated.

CHRISTIAN MAZZALAI: There was a moment of tension. He was very kind but he wanted to be too much a part of it.

THOMAS MARS: He was mixing music for commercials. For a month he mixed this awkward Dior perfume commercial with Johnny Depp, the one where he buries his jewelry in the ground like treasure. It's very possible that it influenced "Drakkar Noir." Somehow, it became this relationship where we were renting his studio in the day, and then once we left Laurent could finally get to work on his real job. If we had all been together the first week, setting up the boundaries, I think it would have been easier.

CHRISTIAN MAZZALAI: Zdar came even less on this album.

THOMAS MARS: We wanted him to make the record but he wanted a challenge, too. He was obsessed with saying "modern"; it had to be modern.

LAURENT BRANCOWITZ: He was more of a guru. More like a philosophical presence and guidance than trying to produce the record.

DECK D'ARCY: He challenged us less.

LAURENT BRANCOWITZ: That's a problem: When you have a little bit of success, people tend to think you don't really need their advice, and so they are slightly less antagonist. It's not the perfect environment for creating.

DECK D'ARCY: Zdar talking about leaving room for failure came out as a guideline. It's probably a reaction to the big success of *Wolfgang*. We were trying to explore what happens on the edge of failing. Maybe this is why *Bankrupt!* sounds a bit aggressive. It's probably an unconscious reaction to this big step we experienced before.

CHRISTIAN MAZZALAI: We wanted to do *Thriller* but with something more dirty. Thomas wanted to call the album *Thriller 2*.

LAURENT BRANCOWITZ: It's one of the rare albums that we never stopped loving, even when we were in our teenage rebellion and listening to My Bloody Valentine. This album marks a key moment where technology and taste were both aligned. It's full of this desire to make something new, and it's totally hybrid between real and fake, technology and real players. It's so big that people forget how good it is.

DECK D'ARCY: Obviously the album came out in a weird way. I'm not sure it's really Michael Jackson at all.

LAURENT BRANCOWITZ: I was reading about how *Thriller* was recorded, and I saw that the console was for sale on eBay. It seemed like it could not be true, but it had to be true because if it was a con, the listing would have been better.

CHRISTIAN MAZZALAI: The text was so crazy. "I got the real Thriller! Yes! The real one! Michael Jackson, yeah!"

LAURENT BRANCOWITZ: It belonged to an American guy from Orange County who ran a Christian label.

CHRISTIAN MAZZALAI: I think the day after Michael Jackson died, he wanted to sell it for a million dollars. And because the listing was so crazy, everyone thought it was fake.

THOMAS MARS: No one was seeing how precious this thing is. Eric Clapton can play a guitar once and auction it for a fortune. This was a unique desk that had been built by the best technical people. So we thought, if we can have it, we want it. It makes any instrument sound great. *Thriller* sounds contemporary: you could put it out tomorrow.

DECK D'ARCY: We felt like detectives trying to find out if it was the real one. We had to call the technicians that worked on it in the '80s, and they had to sign papers to verify it. It lasted, like, three months before we were sure it was the right one. We ended up buying it for fifteen thousand dollars. Maybe it would be in the trash if we hadn't bought it. It's three meters long, and heavy like a car.

CHRISTIAN MAZZALAI: The shipping was more expensive than the desk. Then we had to repair it because it was very old and not in good shape. We had one guy working on it for months. Only four of the tracks worked.

THOMAS MARS: We sent Peter who we knew from Roman's production company to film an interview with the owner of the desk.

PETER J. BRANDT: We interviewed Christopher Lee Clayton—or Clayton Rose, as he sometimes called himself—just after the console was removed from his studio to be shipped to France. He showed us around this place where he now exclusively records praise and worship music. The control room was in total disarray. He had a lot of stories about the L.A. recording scene over the decades. It was evident that a lot of his experiences with sex, drugs, and rock and roll had pushed him towards his newfound faith. He told us that when people listen to the Christian music he was now working on, "Instead of wanting to put a .38 to the side of your head, you'll want to get down on your knees and pray."

LAURENT BRANCOWITZ: In the world of recording equipment, this was maybe the ultimate talisman. We believe in the magical power of objects. Deck is more minimalist. He's very afraid of possessions. So for him having tons of equipment is a nightmare.

DECK D'ARCY: I love instruments and I love sound, but buying the desk was such a big deal. I felt a bit ashamed we had to ship it to us and not go to it. It's memorabilia that I'm not into. I like to press the keys of a keyboard, and if it sounds good, then great. I don't care who it belonged to. Although this wasn't just memorabilia, it had been specifically designed for the engineer to create a unique sound.

CHRISTIAN MAZZALAI: We used it in the end on vocals and on guitar. It was a very long process. I still cannot believe it. I don't know if I'm objective or not, but it was worth it. Everything we recorded on it was magical.

THOMAS MARS: We used the *Thriller* desk for mixing, but the voice was still recorded with a ten dollar conference microphone. The contrast is appealing.

LAURENT BRANCOWITZ: We were really focused. I was working all the time, or trying to do research into new recording techniques, new things for shows. I was a very positive source on this album, pushing endlessly. On other albums, it wasn't like that.

THOMAS MARS: My memory is of months trying to figure out how to keep the charm of the demo. Hours of recreating the first take.

DECK D'ARCY: On *Wolfgang, Bankrupt!*, and *Ti Amo*, we worked on all the songs at once, so they evolved together. We finished them all in the last months, which was good in a way, but mentally it drives you a bit crazy. It was a bit difficult to see the direction from one song.

CHRISTIAN MAZZALAI: It was very complex for me as the archivist. There was too much information. We had many, many raw products, like two hundred bridges. It was a very extreme technique, but an interesting experimentation.

LAURENT BRANCOWITZ: This record is very dense in terms of structure. There's a lot of key changes and a lot of tempo changes, things that usually you don't do when you want to satisfy the listener's immediate pleasure.

DECK D'ARCY: For some reason, *Bankrupt!* doesn't groove at all. It doesn't really make you want to dance. Dance music is about one extended loop, and *Bankrupt!* is like six- or seven-part songs, complicated structures. We didn't want to use this Maria beat again because it had been a success on the album before, so we had to do something radically different.

LAURENT BRANCOWITZ: We should have thought about the groove. It's very important; the body response is part of the magic of music.

THOMAS MARS: I liked the idea that you create something positive from the disgusting, the negative. Before we wanted one percent of that. On *Bankrupt!*,

Glenn-Jim- NOTARY

(33)

☆ ENCLOSED

From: J
& G
Authenti
Re: The
Co

n FiTzPATrick
nn Phoenix
Tion LeTTers
hriller MJ
sole

we wanted fifty percent, just to see how far we could go.

LAURENT BRANCOWITZ: There's a lot of cynicism. It wasn't just the U.S., it was another movement of the world and of social media. We had to fight against all this, so this record is a dystopian world of synthetic smells. It's very full and very compressed and a bit claustrophobic. Even if we didn't want to make a statement, it just happened to be a strong reaction.

THOMAS MARS: "Bourgeois" came out spontaneously, and I could see how it was something new for us. There was a sense of danger: *Are we going to sing a chorus with a French word?* Somehow it gave us goosebumps so we had no choice but to stay with it. It's the last word that French people would want to sing. There's no way you're going to sing "bourgeois" as a chorus.

LAURENT BRANCOWITZ: When we wrote "Entertainment," we were picturing the national funeral of a North Korean leader, millions of people in the streets crying. So we had this vision of dictatorship mixed with the question of what entertainment is.

THOMAS MARS: Coachella book the headliners one year before. So we had to say yes to headlining the 2013 festival. It gave us this deadline, which is not how we work.

DECK D'ARCY: We absolutely wanted to release the album before the festival because you don't really feel comfortable going on tour with no new material.

CHRISTIAN MAZZALAI: It was fantastic, very risky, that's what we liked about it. We thought it would be good to put an artistic deadline, otherwise we could keep working for another year.

LAURENT BRANCOWITZ: That was a big mistake for our sanity. The deadline was coming and we were being very slow. The timing was really bad. Finishing the record, being ready to do a good show in front of a lot of thousands of people, it was not comfortable at all. We were working all the time to finish. Chris would talk very fast just to gain a few seconds.

CHRISTIAN MAZZALAI: It was a gigantic puzzle. Everything was blurry until the last second. The last week everything came into resolution: maximalist pop music, very fast, very hot. Dirty, with complex, adventurous songs.

PHILIPPE ZDAR: It wasn't aggressive like Slayer, but aggressively saturated. In the end, there was a little fight about that. We never really fight. But I wasn't sure about this. It was the first time we had tension. We were all tired.

DECK D'ARCY: I don't remember fighting with Zdar, but the record company thought the album was too distorted. We finished mixing at 10 a.m. one day, and at noon, we were in the rehearsal studio for the tour. That was exhausting.

PHILIPPE ZDAR: I think if there hadn't been the Coachella deadline, I would have gone away for two weeks, they would have slept. But, in the end, nobody slept. We worked like maniacs. Nobody was agreeing on the sound, the saturation, these little details. It's always nano-details that change everything in life.

DECK D'ARCY: *Bankrupt!* was a natural title because we felt so drained.

PHILIPPE ZDAR: We basically chose this title one hour before doing the sleeve. The day we decided on *Wolfgang*, it was a lot easier to finish the album. You can think, "Is this *Wolfgang Amadeus Phoenix*?" You can refer to your title.

CHRISTIAN MAZZALAI: We knew we wanted not to destroy success, but to play with it. That's why we called it *Bankrupt!*, in a positive way. It was a feeling of being totally free creatively.

DECK D'ARCY: We added the exclamation mark to make it seem more positive.

LAURENT BRANCOWITZ: The fruit was a really good cover for this album. It was like an Andy Warhol type of commentary.

THOMAS MARS: We thought "Entertainment" was really solid. I wanted that to be the first song. We asked J Mascis to cover it, and a lot of the reactions were that it was far better than the original. I remember feeling like this is going to be harder to connect. It's nice to feel disconnected. It's a form of comfort.

LAURENT BRANCOWITZ: We knew the album was very hard to swallow. And the themes were not like this sweet candy that people would maybe have liked. I thought the songs were really strong, so I thought it could have worked better.

THOMAS MARS: From the beginning, we were used to going from one country to the other and having different responses. Even on *Wolfgang*, we were already has-beens in Norway because *Alphabetical* was such a success there. There's always been the other side, so I don't really look back, which I think is healthy.

LAURENT BRANCOWITZ: Coachella is like the Olympics of our type of music, especially back then. We love those big, outdoor shows at night. There's something biblical about them. This one would have been the biggest one we had ever done.

DECK D'ARCY: It was not the same Coachella as we used to do when we were younger. It was more the big machine it became, the V.I.P. area in front of the stage.

THOMAS MARS: To have a good show, sometimes it takes thirty shows before.

We knew that Coachella would be maybe our seventh show. We tried to have more before that but we were behind schedule.

LAURENT BRANCOWITZ: We had a very ambitious vision of the show and we didn't have the perfect team. Just one or two weeks before the show there were big problems with the lighting. It created a lot of tension. We were looking for something that would make it unforgettable for us.

DECK D'ARCY: We were looking for a guest because it's funny to have a guest. Everyone was expecting the Daft guys so we had to do something different. We thought about bringing the *Star Wars* robots instead because Thomas knew George Lucas through Sofia.

THOMAS MARS: People were certain Daft Punk were coming. So we knew that no matter what, we were going to disappoint that expectation. I thought we could ask to have R2–D2 and C–3PO. But then it felt like a strange idea to have two robots, just not the right ones.

LAURENT BRANCOWITZ: We had this idea of mixing R. Kelly with our song. Aesthetically, he is very different from us, so the contrast was interesting. We had this idea of mixing his song with ours, so we sent him a demo. He always replied very fast, singing on top of it, or changing the structure. Our contact was purely musical.

DECK D'ARCY: He doesn't fly, so he spent seven days coming from Chicago on his tour bus to do a three-minute show.

LAURENT BRANCOWITZ: When we went on stage, he was still stuck in traffic. When the moment came that he was supposed to appear, we didn't know if he would.

CHRISTIAN MAZZALAI: He appeared onstage while we were playing and then we saw him backstage for a few minutes. Then he went back in his tour bus.

THOMAS MARS: Musically, it was so tempting: two worlds that had nothing to do with each other. What we regret is not letting ourselves be more informed. In hindsight, this was an obvious mistake that we're sorry for.

THOMAS MARS: The name *Bankrupt!* felt pretty obvious. Because *Wolfgang* was so big, the infrastructure for this album was automatically bigger, even though the record turned out not to be. It's getting bigger but it's not massive. And you know it's not going to last, so it's bittersweet. People around us knew it. But we were in denial. On *Wolfgang*, you'd be in Kansas City and there were all these new faces from radio telling you you were number one. On *Bankrupt!*, these people disappeared. We knew that people were not as excited about the

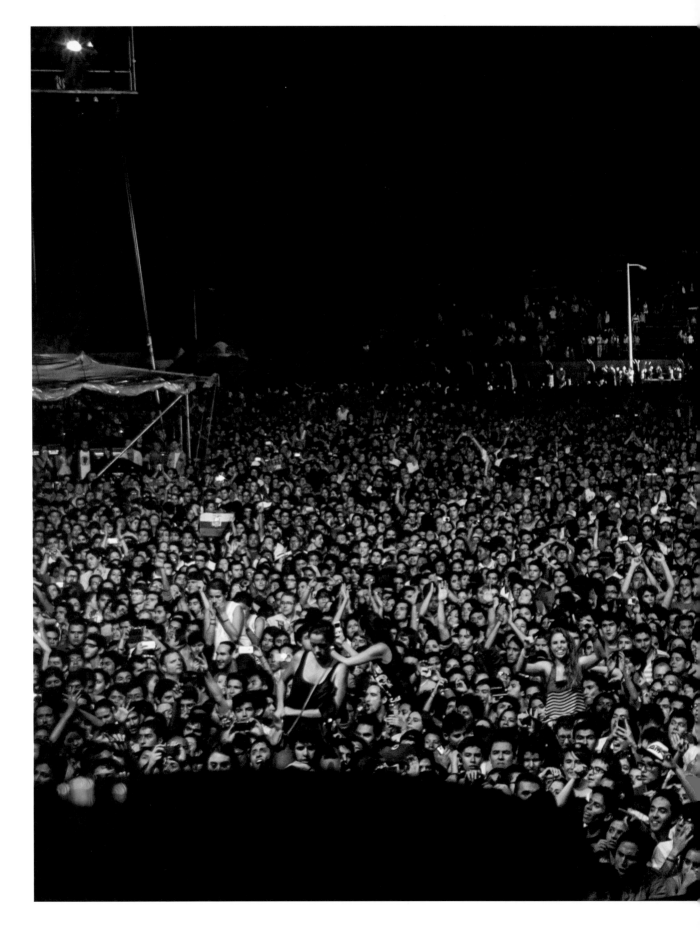

record. We were proud of it, but we knew when we played live that there was no hit that everyone wanted to hear.

DECK D'ARCY: We did two or three shows in Australia for a brand-new festival. We were tricked. It was meant to be a good lineup with other bands like Arctic Monkeys. But we ended up being the only band on an E.D.M. music festival. It was the worst situation.

LAURENT BRANCOWITZ: It was the beginning of the peak of E.D.M., which was the most frightening moment because you have this feeling it will last forever. We were touring in front of thousands of E.D.M. frat boys from Australia, very tan, very muscular, a lot of testosterone.

CHRISTIAN MAZZALAI: Our fans didn't want to go to this festival that was very far from our music. It was like the end of civilization, everyone totally wrecked on drugs, screaming, "*Let's get fucking wasted!*" Violent, stupid boys.

LAURENT BRANCOWITZ: In a way, it was the perfect setting for *Bankrupt!*. A commentary about the modern world and its most horrible aspects.

THOMAS MARS: You would watch the same show played over and over by different guys: "Seven Nation Army," a Rihanna remix. We couldn't relate.

LAURENT BRANCOWITZ: Behind the testosterone I could feel some kind of universal melancholy. The music is about building expectations and then a big disappointment, the drop. It is a metaphor for life: a big anticipation then disappointment. Any cultural moment that is based totally on these emotions is bound to fail at some point because it's too cruel. Usually you try to make the disappointing part of your artwork as minimal as possible, whereas in this art form, the center is based on disappointment, in a way. I guess all those teenagers learn this, and then they don't want to repeat the mistake forever. That's my hope.

CHRISTIAN MAZZALAI: But we met Gesaffelstein for the first time, and we had crazy fun times with him, and Brodinski, too—they are French, they explained E.D.M. to us. I learned many musical tricks: eight bars up, the kick comes in, people scream for one and a half seconds, then you go down again. I stayed at the shows at long as possible because I was fascinated. It was such a disaster, we had to learn something otherwise it would be too much of a waste. We took one or two of these things into *Ti Amo*. On the song "Ti Amo," there's a very cheap E.D.M. riser. It was so far from our music, but we loved this.

LAURENT BRANCOWITZ: Those memories are the best in retrospect. You always remember those moments on holiday where you are lost or trapped in a very bad motel.

THOMAS MARS: We played Vegas. Every show in Vegas is strange because you don't know if it's day or night. We were playing in front of a pool; they empty the pool and the crowd stands in it. People watch from balconies sixty floors up. We're soundchecking and people are shouting out the names of songs they want to hear, so we play them. But then someone official is pointing at us and saying we have to stop because this couple is having sex on a balcony. It was one of those moments when you're not sure what you're doing. You realize it's less about the music.

LAURENT BRANCOWITZ: We went to see Al Green in his small church in Memphis. He's a preacher, but he sings and has a band.

CHRISTIAN MAZZALAI: It was a tiny church, unbelievable. Then you do the line, "What's your name? Chris! Where do you come from? Paris! God bless you, Chris!" Everyone was blessed by Al Green. He left in a black car. We were in the parking lot waiting for a taxi to go back to our hotel: he waved at us from his car. This vision for me will live on until I die. It was beautiful.

LAURENT BRANCOWITZ: Those moments were really amazing.

CHRISTIAN MAZZALAI: My favorite aftershow was in Japan. I love Japan. In 2006, I moved to the Japanese district in Paris. In my building, there was a grocery run by an old guy who I would see every day. He imported all the best sake in Europe. He sold seaweed to Michelin restaurants. This old guy became a big friend. I called him *maître*; he was like my mentor. He came to Japan with us for *Bankrupt!* and we spent many crazy nights where he would invite sake brewers. I learned so much from him. You can be in front of a beautiful piece of art, but if you don't make any input, nothing will happen. The listener has to add something to the art. I wanted him to write the liner notes to *Bankrupt!* but he passed away.

LAURENT BRANCOWITZ: He was a very charismatic figure. He introduced us to a kind of Japanese poetry, a way of seeing things, *wabi-sabi*.

CONSO

QE THEATER, VANCOUVER 28 MARCH 2013

ENTERTAINMENT OCHAFUZZ

LISZTOMANIA

LASSO x 11 13 | REF= 7

LONG DISTANCE CALL CAPO post intro

THE REAL THING CAPO sur fin LdC

FENCES

GIRLFRIEND

DRAKKAR NOIR

CHLOROFORM PORTA puis MIDI 11

S.O.S. IN BEL AIR REMETTRE MIDI 10 puis PORTA

SUNSKRUPT! xx7 | MICHAEL xx7 | ACRES

TRYING TO BE COOL E Am G CC FA

OBLIQUE CITY FIN MIDI 11

ARMISTICE INTRO 7 REF 8 FIN 5

BOURGEOIS Legato

1901

—

DON'T xx 8 - 10

ROME "ROME, ROME, ROME" = 10

ENTERT (G#)

*Après le spectacle, rendez-vous
à l'espace cocktail de la salle*
pour boire un verre !*

Tendrement,

PHŒNIX ♥

THOMAS MARS: At the end of the tour we were really happy that we got our core audience back. We won the French equivalent of the Grammy, the Victoires de la Musique. They're so cheap, they give you just one statue. It used to look like a pair of balls, but they had changed it by the time we won. So I asked my dad's friend, this forger in Provence, to cut it in four. We each took a piece. I think Chris lost his. It's the perfect *Bankrupt!* trophy.

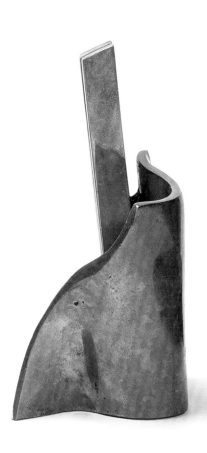

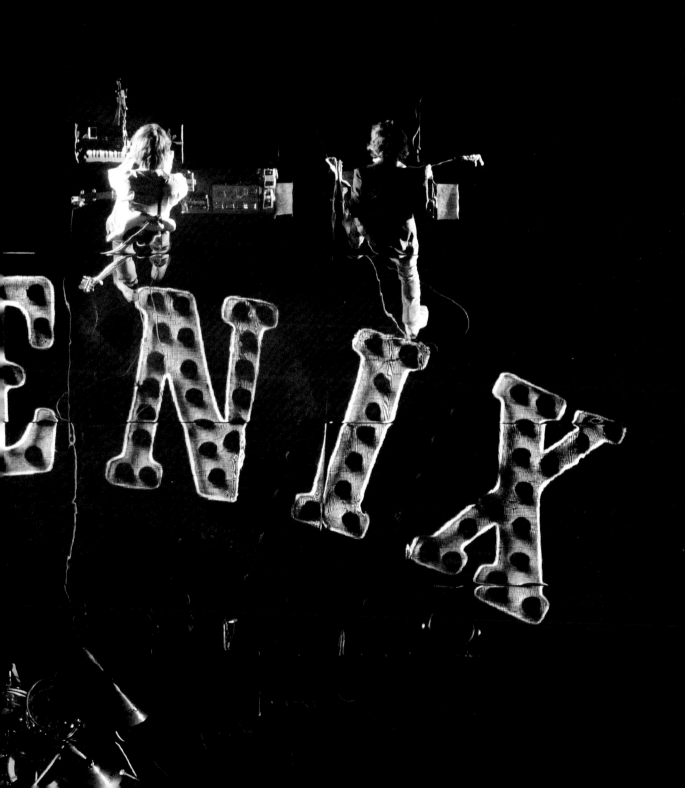

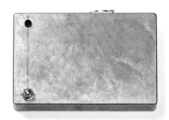

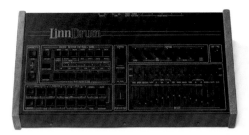

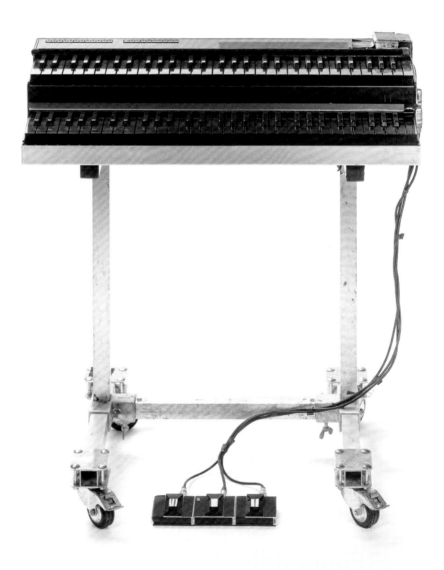

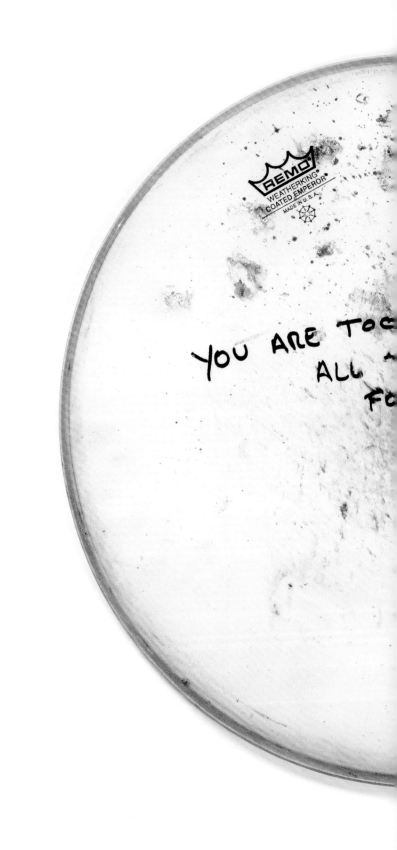

TI AMO

2017

Other voices: CHAG BARATIN, business, production, and tour manager. ROB COUDERT, keyboards. PIERRICK DEVIN, co-producer. BENOÎT ROUSSEAU, la Gaîté Lyrique. PHILIPPE ZDAR, guru.

LAURENT BRANCOWITZ: *Ti Amo* is really built around this idea of trying to erase what's dark and to focus on what's light.

CHRISTIAN MAZZALAI: We wanted to enjoy Paris and family life after all this touring. We visited la Gaîté Lyrique, where they had a studio under the roof. We stayed there for two years. It was very different from all the other places we'd been before, because for the first time we were not separate from the outside world.

THOMAS MARS: It's in the middle of this strange digital museum that's very French because it's trying to be so many things at once. It has a venue, small exhibits, a movie theater; people work there on strange, technological concepts. Almost every night there's a show, so at 5 p.m., we could watch soundcheck. It was refreshing not to be isolated.

DECK D'ARCY: We liked feeling like we had an office job because we never had them. It was the opposite of a studio vibe, a virgin place in that no significant records had been done there before.

PIERRICK DEVIN: The studio looked like an open-plan office.

BENOÎT ROUSSEAU: It was very unusual for Phoenix to come and record here. But they actually fit really well in that environment. They gave a workshop for middle-school kids who had learned their songs.

THOMAS MARS: Towards the beginning of the process, I got a text from Laurent, the owner of T.L.C., that said, "I hope you're home safe," with nothing else, so I knew there must be something going on. Deck, Branco, and I were home.

CHRISTIAN MAZZALAI: The night of the Bataclan attack, I was at la Gaîté Lyrique watching a band. We had to all stay there for a long, long, long time on security lockdown. It was very shocking.

BENOÏT ROUSSEAU: Le Bataclan is just a few blocks away from la Gaîté Lyrique.

LAURENT BRANCOWITZ: I had an old friend that was organizing the event at the Bataclan. There was an element of not knowing who was safe and who wasn't. We knew people who were injured—not close friends, but close to our scene.

CHRISTIAN MAZZALAI: Very dark times. In a way, we had to do music to exorcise this thing that was so shocking.

LAURENT BRANCOWITZ: Trying to understand how it would be to write this music during this period was a very dark moment. You would open your news feed and be afraid of what you were going to see. There was this feeling of anguish. I would go home and see the news, and compare it to the music we had just recorded. It really didn't make sense.

THOMAS MARS: You feel useless. You're not sure if the only thing you're good at is actually useful for the moment. The idea that it's the four of us making this, and that if we like it then eventually someone else will like it—this whole concept falls apart. The connection between what you're doing and where it's supposed to go feels embarrassing. It's like the satellite that they sent into space with Blur's "Song 2." I thought that was the most shameful thing—it showed how immature and pompous humanity is that, ten years ago, we thought we lived in a great time, that this was our generation's anthem, and so aliens should know it. Somehow being in the studio then felt the same.

DECK D'ARCY: I'm not sure we were that conscious of the atmosphere. We didn't really have any concepts.

LAURENT BRANCOWITZ: This period was really tense around the world, with the migrant crisis in the Mediterranean, and especially in Paris. But the strange thing is that we were creating very happy music. At first, that felt very disturbing. But later I realized that maybe it was just what we needed, and that maybe some other people out there needed a universe that was more simple.

CHRISTIAN MAZZALAI: Serge Gainsbourg wrote his happy songs in dark times when Brigitte Bardot left him, and he wrote his saddest songs when he was a happy father with a family with Jane Birkin. So I think it's very common to work in the opposite direction. In Paris, everyone was still *en terrasse*. Life goes on, it's the reality.

LAURENT BRANCOWITZ: I think we were all yearning for something light and fresh and naïve; honest emotions. Exactly the opposite of *Bankrupt!*. No cynicism. We wanted to give a sense of hope. We really never thought about it in those terms, but if I analyze it now, I think that's where our instinct pushed us.

CHRISTIAN MAZZALAI: It led us to my and Branco's summer holidays in Italy. Our motto was to do something very light; that the emotion should be very pure, very calming, *candide*, innocent.

LAURENT BRANCOWITZ: Chris and I have a very strong memory based on the smell of our aunt's house in the mountains, the wood-burning fire, and soup. It was the place we saw our father's cousins playing guitar late at night, witnessing this magic of music for the first time. A private mythology. Strangely, last time we were in Korea, we could smell this exact thing. Chris and I were smelling this perfume, and the Korean guys in the restaurant didn't get it.

CHRISTIAN MAZZALAI: The link with our father was very strong. My dad passed away at the beginning of *Wolfgang*. We had two years to digest it, it was such a shock. Even when someone is talking Italian in the street in Paris, I still follow them a bit, just to hear the music.

LAURENT BRANCOWITZ: Maybe there was some connection to our father, but we didn't really do it consciously. We were interested in a golden age of Italian culture, which would have been from the period when our parents were young.

THOMAS MARS: I was influenced by the brothers. I think they wanted to remember their youth, and Deck and I were were embracing their world. It was refreshing to discover it through their eyes.

DECK D'ARCY: I think nostalgia has always been in our D.N.A. Maybe less on *Bankrupt!*. But even *Wolfgang* and *United* are nostalgic. It can come out in many different ways.

ROB COUDERT: This record sounds more like, "Fuck it, let's go on holiday and make love!" It's the sweet side side of Phoenix, which I love the most. Tenderness is something they're good at.

LAURENT BRANCOWITZ: Our father left Italy in '66, so he missed a lot of really good things that we discovered later. We tried to dig very seriously into this little goldmine, like Lucio Battisti. There's a charm and a tenderness to his music, and the lyrics are really deep. It's the texture of the emotion that's important, something that I couldn't really find in any other culture. For us it meant a lot. Maybe we had exhausted the catalogue of old masters. We needed something fresher and maybe less intimidating.

CHRISTIAN MAZZALAI: Like Serge Gainsbourg, Battisti was different from English or American pop. Another god that few people know, and one of the most beautiful gods. He used so many techniques and themes that no one else used. He's a very unique artist. In Italy, he's as famous as the Pope. He made no compromises. He did no interviews, no shows, just music, but at the same time very mainstream. Very interesting.

THOMAS MARS: Roman asked me to make a playlist for a dinner party in Napa. I put on a Lucio Battisti song. As it's playing, the chef comes out of the kitchen, full-on crying, asking, "Who played Battisti?" I realized the connection that Battisti has with Italy is so strong.

PIERRICK DEVIN: In the studio, we had office schedules. Christian was in charge of assigning tasks for each workday. He called himself "*l'assistant-réal*"—the assistant director—the essential job on a movie set to get things done.

THOMAS MARS: We were trying out things and all four of us would instantly agree or disagree. We were going in the same direction. I remember singing "Fior di Latte," and the other three's eyes lit up. We were excited because it was really strange. In terms of commercial appeal, it's not a good idea to have a chorus in Italian. It's obscure. But it was really appealing.

CHRISTIAN MAZZALAI: We thought it was virgin territory. We knew it was exciting for us, at least. I'm totally not objective because of my father passing away.

LAURENT BRANCOWITZ: We all felt it was full of electricity. Fior di latte is a typical Italian ice cream flavor. It's a very precise memory of pure joy from when we were kids. But I also think this song is a cheesy, erotic metaphor. And we enjoyed this aspect of it. We were thinking about that time when your emotions are totally pure, when you are not judgmental. An age when things are pure and innocent.

THOMAS MARS: There are a few words that I am saying wrong, like on "Via Veneto," the emphasis is in the wrong place. "Fior di latte" was said with a French accent, but we wanted to keep it. It's honest, and the charm of it is in the distortion, the distance. When we were singing in Italian, we were making sure that it was still us because we were still traumatised by *yé-yé*, French people singing American songs and having jukeboxes in their house, renting Mustangs in California. It was *taquin*, mischievous.

CHRISTIAN MAZZALAI: Our father was working on Via Veneto. He worked at a very big hotel when he was young, in '65, '66. Fellini was also living very close to Via Veneto. We loved this idea—we thought it would be more interesting to render a vision of Via Veneto, not the real one. That's what we did on *Ti Amo*—the fantasy version.

THOMAS MARS: We take a lot of joy with doing things that are not in trend. Our album is *Ti Amo* and now Italy is going backwards again. I don't think it's in denial, it just shows an alternative.

LAURENT BRANCOWITZ: We knew it was a very strong reaction against the popular mood. We are a product of the postwar European dream. Our parents come from different European cities. So if Europe is kind of collapsing, I guess it has some kind of effect on us.

THOMAS MARS: "Role Model" is sort of about Trump, but it was not on purpose. It was impossible to take these thoughts and feelings out of your life.

CHRISTIAN MAZZALAI: The darkness in it is pretty obvious.

THOMAS MARS: We were very introspective. It was about how far the four of us can go because we know we're gonna take a lot of pleasure playing those songs together. It has a more positive message than *Bankrupt!*, but the alienation and the confrontational aspect is even stronger. I don't know if people understood that. "J-Boy" was risky because it's another niche reference—French people reappropriating hip-hop in the '80s. Super white guys talking because they can't really rap. It was a guilty pleasure.

CHRISTIAN MAZZALAI: Zdar only came three times, but those three times were key moments. He wanted us to mix ourselves, do everything ourselves, so that's what we did. He was always saying, "*jeté, jeté*"—it's like when you just throw something, you don't control it at all.

THOMAS MARS: What's great in these words is that they mean something to him, but they have a different meaning for us. It's a word that's empty enough for us to find something in common. For me, it means spontaneous, not calculated, bold.

DECK D'ARCY: *Bankrupt!* was very complex. In a way it was a bit like *Alphabetical*—it could be two different bands with the same singer. The *Ti Amo* process was not as painful, but it was similarly layered. We talked about minimalism even if it's absolutely not minimalist, but maybe on the Phoenix scale it is.

THOMAS MARS: I started to feel during *Bankrupt!*, but even more during *Ti Amo*, that we didn't need the instruments we were surrounding ourselves with anymore. We had the same freedom that we felt when we were making *United* when you could suddenly make an album in your bedroom: now you could make the first scratches of an album with nothing. What we need is a big table and chairs, good speakers, and there's no need for anything else. I have a cheap Chinese conference microphone that costs ten bucks. That's the new liberating feeling of this record. There's not even pressure of setting up. You're just working, waiting for the genie to come.

LAURENT BRANCOWITZ: We sampled a lot of our own rhythm tracks from the past. Any time I would find a piece of music with good rhythm, I would sample it. There's a lot of dance music from the early '80s on there. We listened to a lot of music from South Africa, Somalia, Ethiopia, Egypt. Dur-Dur Band is a Somalian band that used a very formidable scale. Those tools were very precious—suddenly a new world opens up for you.

DECK D'ARCY: We lost the groove on *Bankrupt!* but I think we got it back on *Ti Amo*.

CHRISTIAN MAZZALAI: We had the keys to every floor of la Gaîté Lyrique, so we could always sneak in to see the bands rehearsing that day. That's how we discovered Dodi El Sherbini, who arranged two songs on *Ti Amo*.

THOMAS MARS: The first time I heard his music, I saw a lot of connections. I felt like I really knew what he grew up listening to. His way of working is totally different from us but very compatible. He makes a song a day. If we give him something, he'll work on it for two hours. He thinks that he can do his best in two hours, and after that, there's no evolution. He understood the fabric of our music really quickly.

BENOÎT ROUSSEAU: They told me that they learned to play by covering every Teenage Fanclub song. I had booked Teenage Fanclub for the concert hall of la Gaîté Lyrique in February 2017, and after the soundcheck I asked if they wanted to say hello to Phoenix. When we arrived in their studio, the Phoenix boys were surprisingly shy. To break the ice, Norman Blake asked if they could listen to what they were recording, and Branco played "Ti Amo." It was the first time someone outside of the band got to hear what they were cooking in the studio.

THOMAS MARS: Sofia was directing an opera in Rome, so we lived there for three months. That came late when we were making the record, and it helped me embrace the fact that I was comfortable with that decision. I hadn't spent a lot of time there before.

PIERRICK DEVIN: Mixing, producing, and overdubbing were done at the same time. It was an exciting process because we were mixing "in the box"—digitally, inside the computer—so we could tweak the mix over and over, like a painter would put a certain color on his canvas one day then another color two weeks after. I think the final version of the song "Ti Amo" was mix thirty-nine.

DECK D'ARCY: It was a fun album to make. At the end, as always, we struggled to admit it was finished, but I really enjoyed the creative process.

LAURENT BRANCOWITZ: This record was very much loved by our friends and family. It's not always like that, but it had an instant impact on those we know very well. Even when the recordings were released to a wider audience, this first impression lasts for a long time.

DECK D'ARCY: I understand why the reception was a bit muted. It's a complicated album, which was not really the vibe at that moment. Music went super minimalist and we went the other way, which is what we have always been doing. Sometimes that clicks with the vibe of the moment, but it's random, the planets aligning. They're aligned because they're not aligned. We have no problem with that. We are a bit jealous of the minimalism sometimes. It would be great to make a song with just two tracks.

CHRISTIAN MAZZALAI: When we were doing our first album, for us we were creating a revolution, and we realized quite fast that, to other people, it's only music. Even when you go to the Louvre, people walk past the masterpieces. It's impossible for people to react the way you want. I think for *Ti Amo*, people don't see the mechanisms, which are very complex, but in a way it's good that they don't see it.

THOMAS MARS: We saw that *Ti Amo* had a cult quality. There were people at the shows that really wanted to hear "Telefono" or "Fior di Latte."

CHRISTIAN MAZZALAI: We asked a friend from childhood to do a study of every stage lighting technique for shows from the Greeks until now. He did almost

an anthropological study. We took the idea for the tour from a French show from the twenties, with girls laying on a painting that was reflected in an overhead mirror, which created the illusion that they were standing. We thought, it's very old but it's still an illusion, so that means it's a very good trick. We spent a year trying to make it work.

CHAG BARATIN: It felt like we turned into a Formula 1 team, with engineers doing calculus and wind-testing. It was a long and stressful year knowing that every time we pull up for a show, my friends were going to play beneath a mirror that weighed four tons. A nightmare.

THOMAS MARS: The tour was really chaotic. It would have been really scary if it was our first tour. We were a bit in the eye of the storm. There were all these disasters, but somehow we always managed to pull things off at the last minute, which wasn't the case on *Bankrupt!*.

CHRISTIAN MAZZALAI: We are always looking for this moment of disaster. With the four of us, we feel this beauty, a leap of faith. You have to go together, and life is more exciting like this.

LAURENT BRANCOWITZ: Bercy arena in Paris was the biggest show we have played in France. It didn't feel like an important achievement to the four of us. But when we started doing music, not a lot of people would have bet on us, I can tell you. So maybe we enjoyed the irony.

PHILIPPE ZDAR: In the end, I think the people who hated them understood that they were here for a long time, and they were respectable.

EPILOGUE

THOMAS MARS: My parents sold their house before Christmas 2017. After *It's Never Been Like That*, we never really went back to make music. It's kind of nice that it's gone. I wish it would have been sold to a guy with kids who could have a space to rehearse, but that's my only regret.

CHRISTIAN MAZZALAI: This house is a big part of our story and now it's not ours anymore. I am not really nostalgic because we are still living the same way. We could be in the most boring city in the world as long as we are together.

DECK D'ARCY: I was very attached to this place. I got married to my wife, Kinga, in the garden where we used to play soccer. Thomas's dad told me, "If you don't get married there, I won't speak to you any more." Then he broke his leg two days before the wedding and couldn't come.

THOMAS MARS: We found tons of weird things when we cleared it out. When we wanted to listen to a mix in our car, we would record on cassette. Because we didn't wanna spend money, you could reuse a pre-recorded cassette if you put tape over the tabs. "If I Ever Feel Better" is on Maria Callas singing *Tosca*. My dad did surveys for a market-testing company, so there's hundreds of these green cassette tapes with voiceovers of people recording commercials for yogurt or soup, with "Too Young" on the other side. We found nametags from our first jobs. We had Branco's old subway card: his picture was Elvis. Somehow he got away with it.

CHRISTIAN MAZZALAI: We found Deck's ski pass with a picture of Beck inside. They looked a lot alike. I found my swimming pool card: a picture of me naked but for my mother's big fur coat.

LAURENT BRANCOWITZ: It's a bit frightening, but we didn't really change a lot.

DECK D'ARCY: Sometimes when we talk about friendship, it's almost embarrassing. People must think we're crazy: we go on vacation together, we tour and work all the time. It almost sounds a bit fake.

THOMAS MARS: The way we function is really hard for people to understand. In the beginning, the British press was always comparing us to the Monkees. When we do interviews, it's always, "How come you never fight?" But there's something way better in the story. Somehow it's not a popular thing to have harmony. It doesn't help your career, really. But that's the reality of our band.

DECK D'ARCY: I don't know whether people understand us but at the same time it doesn't matter—for them, for us, or for the music we make. There have been so many eras: Sometimes we felt we were understood pretty well, sometimes not at all. Sometimes we are surprised the crowd is there, but they're here, so, cool!

CHRISTIAN MAZZALAI: We are in our forties now, and sometimes people come up to me in the street saying they've been following us since they were born, or that their kids grew up listening to us. We are just aging, but we are still learning, we are still *candide*. I think what I like the most is that on my own, I am nothing, and then the power of the exchange between us, the mystery of the chemistry, that's something which is very strong.

THOMAS MARS: In every band documentary, they hate each other. It's so strange. Even *A Star Is Born*—the way people tell stories about music, it has to be doomed. I remember the Beatles wanting to buy four connecting islands in Greece with one in the middle that would be the studio. I think they were joking about how being recluses was the only way they could survive, or maybe it was a real idea. But I would want that.

LAURENT BRANCOWITZ: We do not really disconnect fun and work, but around the start of this album, I visited Salvador Dalí's home in Spain and I realized that you can put a lot of art into your life as well. Dalí bought a small fisherman's house when he became more famous. It's this little cosmos he built for himself around the sea. Eating sea urchins, floating in his bay. That's my new state of mind. I want to be a guy who eats a sea urchin every day. For the first time in our lives, we are trying to follow the path of least resistance and see where it leads us.

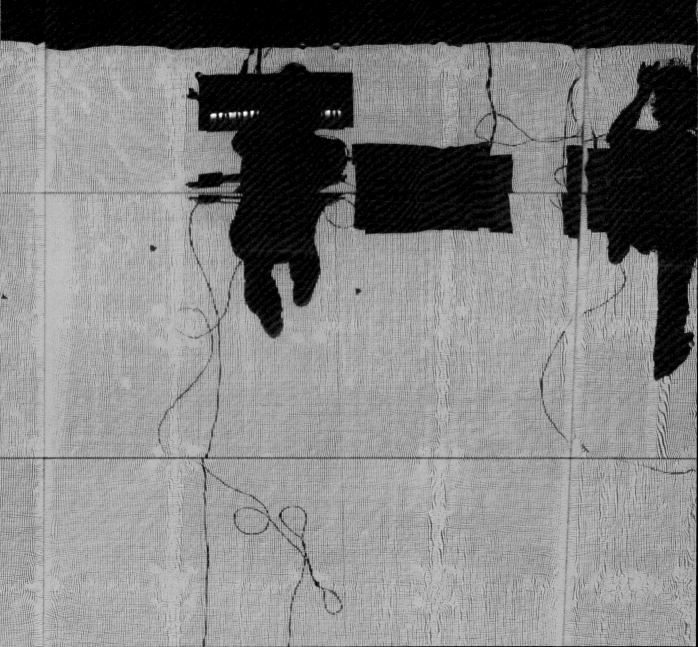

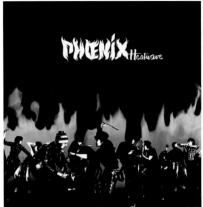

PARTY TIME / CITY LIGHTS

HEATWAVE

UNITED

1997
7-inch single
Label: Ghettoblaster (Ghetto01)
    A. Party Time
    B. City Lights

1998
Air – Kelly Watch The Stars
(American Girls Remix Par Phoenix)
Remix by Phoenix
Label: Source, Virgin Records

Teri Moïse – Il Sait (Phoenix Remix)
Remix by Phoenix
Label: Source, Virgin Records

1999
12-inch single
Label: Source, Virgin Records
    A. Heatwave
    B. I Love You (Cruz Esteban Remix)

Morgan – Miss Parker (Morgan vs Phoenix)
Remix by Phoenix
Label: Source, Virgin Records

2000
Album
Label: Source, Virgin Records, Astralwerks (US)
    1. School's Rules
    2. Too Young
    3. Honeymoon
    4. If I Ever Feel Better
    5. Party Time
    6. On Fire
    7. Embuscade
    8. Summer Days
    9. Funky Square Dance
    (Parts One, Two, Three)
    10. Definitive Breaks

Alternative versions:
    Too Young (Final Edit)
    If I Ever Feel Better (Edit)

2003
Rob – Never Enough (Phoenix Remix)
Remix by Phoenix
Label: Source, Virgin Records
Never released, promotional CD copy only

ALPHABETICAL

LIVE! THIRTY DAYS AGO

IT'S NEVER BEEN LIKE THAT

2004
Album
Label: Source, Virgin Records, Astralwerks (US)
1. Everything Is Everything
2. Run Run Run
3. I'm An Actor
4. Love For Granted
5. Victim Of The Crime
6. (You Can't Blame It On) Anybody
7. Congratulations
8. If It's Not With You
9. Holding On Together
10. Alphabetical
11. Congratulations Revisited
Bonus : The Diary Of Alphabetical
(Early Demos & Studio Footage)

Alternative versions:
Everything Is Everything (Instrumental)
Everything Is Everything (A Capella)
Run Run Run (Edit)
Run Run Run (SBN Acoustic Session)
(You Can't Blame It On) Anybody
(Radio Edit)
I'm An Actor (One-Take Version)
Love For Granted (Acoustic Mix)

2004
Live Album
Label: Source, Virgin Records, Astralwerks (US)
1. Run Run Run (Live)
2. Victim Of The Crime (Live)
3. Too Young (Live)
4. I'm An Actor (Live)
5. Alphabetical (Live)
6. Funky Square Dance (Live)
7. (You Can't Blame It On) Anybody
(Live)
8. Everything Is Everything (Live)
9. If I Ever Feel Better (Live)
10. Love For Granted (Live)

2006
Album
Label: Source, Virgin Records, Astralwerks (US)
1. Napoleon Says
2. Consolation Prizes
3. Rally
4. Long Distance Call
5. One Time Too Many
6. Lost And Found
7. Courtesy Laughs
8. North
9. Sometimes In The Fall
10. Second To None

Alternative version:
Consolation Prizes (Extended Version)

Diet Of The Heart
Demo track
Label: EMI Toshiba Japan
Released exclusively in Japan (album bonus)

Live 2006
iTunes live EP
1. Napoleon Says (Live)
2. Rally (Live)
3. Sometimes In The Fall (Live)
4. Second To None (Live)

2007
Où Boivent Les Loups
Track written for Sofia Coppola's
Marie-Antoinette Original Film Score
Label: EMI Toshiba Japan
Released exclusively in Japan (It's Never Been
Like That album reissue)

WOLFGANG AMADEUS PHOENIX

BANKRUPT!

ALONE ON CHRISTMAS DAY

2009
Album
Label: Ghettoblaster, Cooperative Music/V2
Records, Glassnote
      1. Lisztomania
      2. 1901
      3. Fences
      4. Love Like A Sunset Part I
      5. Love Like A Sunset Part II
      6. Lasso
      7. Rome
      8. Countdown
      9. Girlfriend
      10. Armistice

Alternative versions:
      Lisztomania (Edit)
      1901 (Home Demo)
      Fences (Home Demo)

The Wolfgang Diaries
47 Sketches from the Wolfgang Amadeus
Phoenix sessions
Released exclusively on vinyl included in
the limited-edition Wolfgang Amadeus Phoenix
"Pizza Box" box set (350 copies)

2010
iTunes Festival: London 2010 EP
Live EP, iTunes exclusive
      1. Lisztomania (Live)
      2. Lasso (Live)
      3. Fences (Live)
      4. Countdown (Live)
      5. Rome (Live)
      6. 1901 (Live)

Sofia Coppola's *Somewhere*
Original Film Score (Unreleased)

2013
Album
Label: Loyauté, Glassnote, Atlantic Records,
Liberator Music
      1. Entertainment
      2. The Real Thing
      3. S.O.S In Bel Air
      4. Trying To Be Cool
      5. Bankrupt!
      6. Drakkar Noir
      7. Chloroform
      8. Don't
      9. Bourgeois
      10. Oblique City

Alternative versions:
      Entertainment (Radio Edit)
      엔터테인먼트
      Trying To Be Cool feat. R. Kelly (Remix)
      S.O.S in Bel Air (Radio Version)
      S.O.S in Bel Air (Live In Austin)
      Bourgeois (Take Away Phoenix)
      Bankrupt?
      The Real Thing (Live In Austin)
      Oblique City (Demo)
      Don't (Live In Austin)
      Drakkar Noir (Demo)

The Bankrupt! Diaries
71 sketches from the Bankrupt! sessions

2015
7-inch single
Beach Boys cover
Label: Loyauté, Glassnote, Atlantic Records,
Liberator Music
      A. Alone On Christmas Day
      B. Alone On Christmas Day
      (Instrumental)

TI AMO

MONOLOGUE

2017
Album
Label: Loyauté, Glassnote, Atlantic Records,
Liberator Music
  1. J-Boy
  2. Ti Amo
  3. Tuttifrutti
  4. Fior Di Latte
  5. Lovelife
  6. Goodbye Soleil
  7. Fleur De Lys
  8. Role Model
  9. Via Veneto
  10. Telefono

Phoenix Spotify Singles
Single, Spotify exclusive
  1. J-Boy (Spotify Singles Version)
  2. Un Peu Menteur (Spotify Singles
  Cover)

2017
Sofia Coppola's *The Beguiled*
Original Film Score (Unreleased)

2018
Ti Amo Diaries
64 sketches from the Ti Amo sessions
Released on cassette and digitally under the
alias "Banque De France"

Lovelife
Single
Label: Loyauté, Glassnote, Atlantic Records,
Liberator Music
Limited edition 7-inch vinyl
  A. Lovelife
  B. Lovelife By Giorgio Poi

2019
10-inch single
Label: Loyauté, Glassnote, Atlantic Records,
Liberator Music
Exclusive Record Store Day limited edition
single-sided heart shaped 7-inch vinyl

CREDITS

First published in the United States of America in 2019 by
Rizzoli International Publications, Inc.
300 Park Avenue South
New York, NY 10010
www.rizzoliusa.com

Publisher: Charles Miers
Editor: Jacob Lehman
Production Manager: Maria Pia Gramaglia
Managing Editor: Lynn Scrabis

Art Direction: Apartamento Studios

Phoenix Management: Simon White, Laurence Muller, Matt Sadie

Printed in Italy

2019 2020 2021 2022 / 10 9 8 7 6 5 4 3 2 1

ISBN: 978-0-8478-6483-6
Library of Congress Control Number: 2019943145

Facebook.com/wearephoenix
Twitter @wearephoenix
Instagram.com/wearephoenix
Youtube.com/user/welovephoenix
Wearephoenix.com

Facebook.com/RizzoliNewYork
Twitter @Rizzoli_Books
Instagram.com/RizzoliBooks
Pinterest.com/RizzoliBooks
Youtube.com/user/RizzoliNY
Issuu.com/Rizzoli